# Grandma's Best-Loved Recipes

Publications International, Ltd.

**Microwave Cooking:** Microwave ovens vary in wattage. Use the cooking times as guidelines and check for doneness before adding more time.

**Preparation/Cooking Times:** Preparation times are based on the approximate amount of time required to assemble the recipe before cooking, baking, chilling or serving. These times include preparation steps such as measuring, chopping and mixing. The fact that some preparations and cooking can be done simultaneously is taken into account. Preparation of optional ingredients and serving suggestions is not included.

# Contents

# Soups & Stews

## POTATO & CHEDDAR SOUP

♥ ♥ ♥

  2  cups water
  2  cups red potatoes, peeled and cut into cubes
  3  tablespoons butter or margarine
  1  small onion, finely chopped
  3  tablespoons all-purpose flour
     Red and ground black pepper to taste
  3  cups milk
  ½  teaspoon sugar
  1  cup shredded Cheddar cheese
  1  cup cubed cooked ham

Bring water to a boil in large saucepan. Add potatoes and cook until tender. Drain, reserving 1 cup liquid, adding water if necessary. Melt butter in saucepan over medium heat. Add onion; cook and stir until tender but not brown. Add flour; season with red and black pepper. Cook 3 to 4 minutes. Gradually add potatoes, reserved liquid, milk and sugar to onion mixture; stir well. Add cheese and ham. Simmer over low heat 30 minutes, stirring frequently. *Do not boil.*                         *Makes 12 servings*

*Potato & Cheddar Soup*

# GAZPACHO

♥ ♥ ♥

2 carrots, peeled
1 seedless cucumber, unpeeled
1 medium tomato
½ red bell pepper, seeded
1 garlic clove, minced
¼ cup scallions, finely chopped
2 cups spicy tomato juice
2 teaspoons sugar
3 tablespoons white vinegar
½ cup water
½ cup tomato sauce
1 can (15 ounces) navy beans, drained and rinsed

Chop carrots, cucumber, tomato and bell pepper into large chunks. Place all ingredients except beans in food processor; process to make chunky purée. Pour mixture into large bowl. Stir in beans. Chill before serving.

*Makes 6 servings*

*Favorite recipe from* **The Sugar Association, Inc.**

*Gazpacho*

# SWEET POTATO AND HAM SOUP

❤ ❤ ❤

  1   tablespoon butter or margarine
  1   small leek, sliced
  1   clove garlic, minced
  ½   pound ham, cut into ½-inch cubes
  2   medium sweet potatoes, peeled and cut into ¾-inch
       cubes
  4   cups low-sodium chicken broth
  ½   teaspoon dried thyme leaves
  2   ounces fresh spinach, rinsed, stemmed and coarsely
       chopped

Melt butter in large saucepan over medium heat. Add leek and garlic. Cook and stir until leek is tender.

Add ham, sweet potatoes, chicken broth and thyme to saucepan. Bring to a boil over high heat. Reduce heat to medium-low; cook 10 minutes or until sweet potatoes are tender.

Stir spinach into soup. Simmer, uncovered, 2 minutes more or until spinach is wilted. Serve immediately.        *Makes 6 servings*

*Sweet Potato and Ham Soup*

# GREEK LEMON AND RICE SOUP

♥ ♥ ♥

2   tablespoons butter
⅓   cup minced green onions with tops
6   cups canned chicken broth
⅔   cup uncooked long grain white rice
4   eggs
    Juice of 1 fresh lemon, or to taste
⅛   teaspoon ground white pepper (optional)

1. Melt butter in 3-quart saucepan over medium heat. Add green onions. Cook and stir about 3 minutes or until green onions are tender.

2. Stir in chicken broth and rice. Bring to a boil over medium-high heat. Reduce heat to low; simmer, covered, 20 to 25 minutes until rice is tender.

3. Beat eggs in medium bowl with wire whisk until well beaten. Add lemon juice and ½ cup broth mixture to bowl. Gradually return lemon juice mixture to broth mixture in saucepan, stirring constantly. Cook and stir over low heat 2 to 3 minutes until broth mixture thickens enough to lightly coat spoon. *Do not boil.*

4. Stir in pepper, if desired.                     *Makes 6 to 8 servings*

*Greek Lemon and Rice Soup*

# CORN AND TOMATO CHOWDER

♥ ♥ ♥

1½ cups peeled and diced plum tomatoes
¾ teaspoon salt, divided
2 ears corn, husks removed
1 tablespoon butter
½ cup finely chopped shallots
1 clove garlic, minced
1 can (12 ounces) evaporated skim milk
1 cup chicken broth
1 tablespoon finely chopped fresh sage
¼ teaspoon ground black pepper
1 tablespoon cornstarch
2 tablespoons cold water

1. Place tomatoes in nonmetal colander over bowl. Sprinkle ½ teaspoon salt on top; toss to mix well. Allow tomatoes to drain at least 1 hour.

2. Meanwhile, cut corn kernels off the cobs into small bowl. Scrape cobs with dull side of knife to extract liquid from cobs into same bowl; set aside. Discard 1 cob; break remaining cob in half.

3. Heat butter in heavy medium saucepan over medium-high heat until melted and bubbly. Add shallots and garlic; reduce heat to low. Cover and cook about 5 minutes or until shallots are tender. Add milk, broth, sage, pepper and reserved corn cob halves. Bring to a boil over high heat. Reduce heat to low; simmer, uncovered, 10 minutes. Remove and discard cob halves.

*continued on page 14*

*Corn and Tomato Chowder*

*Corn and Totato Chowder, continued*

4. Add corn with liquid; return to a boil over medium-high heat. Reduce heat to low; simmer, uncovered, 15 minutes more. Dissolve cornstarch in water; add to chowder, mixing well. Stir until thickened. Remove from heat; stir in drained tomatoes and remaining ¼ teaspoon salt. Spoon into bowls.

*Makes 6 appetizer servings*

# DIJON HAM AND LENTIL SOUP

♥ ♥ ♥

| | |
|---|---|
| 1 | cup finely chopped onion |
| ¾ | cup finely chopped green bell pepper |
| ½ | cup finely chopped carrot |
| 1 | clove garlic, minced |
| 1 | bay leaf |
| 2 | (14½-fluid ounce) cans chicken broth or lower sodium chicken broth |
| 1 | (14½-ounce) can stewed tomatoes |
| 1¼ | cups water |
| 1 | cup diced ham |
| ¾ | cup dry lentils |
| ½ | cup GREY POUPON® COUNTRY DIJON® Mustard |

In large saucepan, combine all ingredients except mustard. Heat to a boil over medium-high heat. Reduce heat; simmer, uncovered, for 1 hour. Stir in mustard. Serve hot.

*Makes 6 servings*

# SHAKER CHICKEN AND NOODLE SOUP

♥ ♥ ♥

13  cups chicken broth, divided
¼  cup dry vermouth
¼  cup butter or margarine
1  cup heavy cream
1  package (12 ounces) egg noodles
1  cup thinly sliced celery
1½  cups water
¾  cup all-purpose flour
2  cups diced cooked chicken
   Salt and ground black pepper to taste
¼  cup finely chopped parsley (optional)

1. Combine 1 cup broth, vermouth and butter in small saucepan. Bring to a boil over high heat. Continue to boil 15 to 20 minutes or until liquid is reduced to ¼ cup and has a syrupy consistency. Stir in cream. Set aside.

2. Bring remaining 12 cups broth to a boil in Dutch oven. Add noodles and celery; cook until noodles are just tender.

3. Combine water and flour in medium bowl until smooth. Stir into broth mixture. Boil 2 minutes, stirring constantly.

4. Stir in reserved cream mixture; add chicken. Season with salt and pepper. Heat just to serving temperature. *Do not boil.* Sprinkle with parsley, if desired.

*Makes 15 servings*

# RAVIOLI SOUP

♥ ♥ ♥

1 package (9 ounces) fresh or frozen cheese ravioli or tortellini
¾ pound hot Italian sausage, crumbled
1 can (14½ ounces) DEL MONTE® Italian Recipe Stewed Tomatoes
1 can (14 ounces) beef broth
1 can (14½ ounces) DEL MONTE® Cut Green Italian Beans, drained
2 green onions, sliced

1. Cook pasta according to package directions; drain.

2. Meanwhile, cook sausage in 5-quart pot over medium-high heat until no longer pink; drain. Add tomatoes, broth and 1¾ cups water; bring to boil.

3. Reduce heat to low; stir in pasta, green beans and green onions. Simmer until heated through. Season with pepper and sprinkle with grated Parmesan cheese, if desired.
*Makes 4 servings*

**Prep and Cook Time:** 15 minutes

*Ravioli Soup*

# SPLIT PEA SOUP

♥ ♥ ♥

1 package (16 ounces) dried green or yellow split peas
1 pound smoked pork hocks *or* 4 ounces smoked sausage
   links, sliced and quartered *or* 1 meaty ham bone
7 cups water
1 medium onion, chopped
2 medium carrots, chopped
¾ teaspoon salt
½ teaspoon dried basil leaves
¼ teaspoon dried oregano leaves
¼ teaspoon black pepper

Rinse peas thoroughly in colander under cold running water, picking out any debris or blemished peas. Place peas, pork hocks and water in 5-quart Dutch oven.

Add onion, carrots, salt, basil, oregano and pepper to Dutch oven. Bring to a boil over high heat. Reduce heat to medium-low; simmer, uncovered, 1 hour 15 minutes or until peas are tender, stirring occasionally. Stir frequently near end of cooking to keep soup from scorching.

Remove pork hocks; cool. Cut meat into bite-size pieces; set aside.

Carefully ladle 3 cups hot soup into food processor or blender; cover and process until mixture is smooth.

Return puréed soup and meat to Dutch oven. (If soup is too thick, add a little water until desired consistency is reached.) Heat through.

*Makes 6 servings*

*Split Pea Soup*

# HEARTY CHICKEN AND RICE SOUP

♥ ♥ ♥

| | |
|---|---|
| 10 | cups chicken broth |
| 1 | medium onion, chopped |
| 1 | cup sliced celery |
| 1 | cup sliced carrots |
| ¼ | cup snipped parsley |
| ½ | teaspoon cracked black pepper |
| ½ | teaspoon dried thyme leaves |
| 1 | bay leaf |
| 1½ | cups chicken cubes (about ¾ pound) |
| 2 | cups cooked rice |
| 2 | tablespoons lime juice |
| | Lime slices for garnish |

Combine broth, onion, celery, carrots, parsley, pepper, thyme and bay leaf in large Dutch oven. Bring to a boil; stir once or twice. Reduce heat; simmer, uncovered, 10 to 15 minutes. Add chicken; simmer, uncovered, 5 to 10 minutes or until chicken is no longer pink in center. Remove and discard bay leaf. Stir in rice and lime juice just before serving. Garnish with lime slices.                                  *Makes 8 servings*

*Favorite recipe from **USA Rice Federation***

*Hearty Chicken and Rice Soup*

# COUNTRY BEAN SOUP

❤ ❤ ❤

1¼ cups dried navy beans or lima beans, rinsed and
     drained
4 ounces salt pork or fully cooked ham, chopped
¼ cup chopped onion
½ teaspoon dried oregano leaves
¼ teaspoon salt
¼ teaspoon ground ginger
¼ teaspoon dried sage
¼ teaspoon ground black pepper
2 cups fat-free (skim) milk
2 tablespoons butter

1. Place navy beans in large saucepan; add enough water to cover beans. Bring to a boil; reduce heat and simmer 2 minutes. Remove from heat; cover and let stand for 1 hour.

2. Drain beans and return to saucepan. Stir in 2½ cups water, salt pork, onion, oregano, salt, ginger, sage and pepper. Bring to a boil; reduce heat. Cover and simmer 2 to 2½ hours or until beans are tender. (If necessary, add more water during cooking.) Add milk and butter, stirring until mixture is heated through and butter is melted. Season with additional salt and pepper, if desired.

*Makes 6 servings*

*Country Bean Soup*

# FENNEL AND POTATO BISQUE

♥ ♥ ♥

3 tablespoons butter or margarine
1 leek, cut into thin slices
3 cups milk
1 tablespoon vegetable bouillon granules
½ teaspoon ground white pepper
⅔ pound fennel bulb with 1-inch stalk, cut into thin slices
2 cups cubed peeled red potatoes
1 cup half-and-half
3 tablespoons dry sherry
2 tablespoons all-purpose flour
4 ounces blue cheese, crumbled
¼ cup plus 2 tablespoons finely chopped toasted walnuts

1. Melt butter in large saucepan over medium heat. Add leek; cook and stir 10 minutes or until tender.

2. Add milk, bouillon granules and pepper. Bring to a boil over medium-high heat. Add fennel and potatoes. Reduce heat to low. Cover and simmer 15 to 20 minutes or until fennel is very tender.

3. Combine half-and-half, sherry and flour in small bowl; whisk until smooth.

4. Stir flour mixture into fennel mixture. Cook over medium heat until mixture thickens, stirring constantly. *Do not boil.*

5. Ladle soup into soup bowls; sprinkle each serving evenly with blue cheese and walnuts. Garnish, if desired. *Makes 4 servings*

*Fennel and Potato Bisque*

# MINESTRONE

❤ ❤ ❤

3 slices bacon, diced
½ cup chopped onion
1 large clove garlic, minced
2 cans (10½ ounces each) beef broth
1½ cups water
2 cans (15½ ounces) Great Northern beans, undrained
1 can (6 ounces) CONTADINA® Tomato Paste
1 teaspoon Italian herb seasoning
¼ teaspoon ground black pepper
2 medium zucchini, sliced
1 package (10 ounces) frozen mixed vegetables
½ cup elbow macaroni, uncooked
½ cup (2 ounces) grated Parmesan cheese (optional)

1. Sauté bacon until crisp in large saucepan. Add onion and garlic; sauté until onion is tender. Add broth, water, beans and liquid, tomato paste, Italian seasoning and pepper.

2. Reduce heat to low; simmer, uncovered, for 10 minutes. Add zucchini, mixed vegetables and macaroni. Return to a boil over high heat, stirring to break up vegetables.

3. Reduce heat to low; simmer for 8 to 10 minutes or until vegetables and macaroni are tender. Sprinkle with Parmesan cheese just before serving, if desired.

*Makes 8 cups*

*Minestrone*

# CORN, BACON & RICE CHOWDER

❤ ❤ ❤

1 package (7.2 ounces) RICE-A-RONI® Rice Pilaf
2 tablespoons margarine or butter
1 can (13¾ ounces) reduced-sodium or regular chicken broth
1½ cups frozen corn *or* 1 can (16 or 17 ounces) whole kernel corn, drained
1 cup milk
1 cup water
½ cup sliced green onions
2 slices crisply cooked bacon, crumbled

1. In 3-quart saucepan, sauté rice-pasta mix in margarine over medium heat, stirring frequently until pasta is lightly browned.

2. Stir in chicken broth and contents of seasoning packet; bring to a boil over high heat.

3. Cover; reduce heat. Simmer 8 minutes.

4. Stir in corn, milk, water and onions. Simmer, uncovered, 10 to 12 minutes, stirring occasionally. Stir in bacon before serving.          *Makes 4 servings*

# TOMATO SOUP

♥ ♥ ♥

        1   tablespoon vegetable oil
        1   cup chopped onion
        2   cloves garlic, coarsely chopped
       ½   cup chopped carrot
       ¼   cup chopped celery
        2   cans (28 ounces each) crushed tomatoes in tomato
             purée
      3½   cups chicken broth
        1   tablespoon Worcestershire sauce
       ½   to 1 teaspoon salt
       ½   teaspoon dried thyme
       ¼   to ½ teaspoon ground black pepper
        2   to 4 drops hot pepper sauce

Heat oil in large Dutch oven over medium-high heat. Add onion and garlic; cook and stir 1 to 2 minutes until onion is soft. Add carrot and celery; cook 7 to 9 minutes until tender, stirring frequently. Stir in tomatoes, broth, Worcestershire sauce, salt, thyme, pepper and pepper sauce. Reduce heat to low. Cover and simmer 20 minutes, stirring frequently.      *Makes 6 servings*

*Grandma's Secret: For a smoother soup, remove from heat and let cool about 10 minutes. Process soup, in food processor or blender, in small batches until smooth. Return soup to Dutch oven; simmer 3 to 5 minutes or until heated through.*

# MULLIGATAWNY SOUP

♥ ♥ ♥

Nonstick cooking spray
2 cups finely chopped carrots
1 cup chopped green bell pepper
2 ribs celery, thinly sliced
½ cup finely chopped onion
3 cloves garlic, minced
¼ cup all-purpose flour
1 to 2 teaspoons curry powder
3 cups fat-free reduced-sodium chicken broth
1 cup 2% (low-fat) milk
1 pound boneless skinless chicken breasts, cooked and
   cut into ½-inch pieces
1 cup chopped seeded tomato
1 medium apple, peeled, cored and sliced
¼ cup uncooked converted rice
½ teaspoon salt
⅛ teaspoon ground black pepper

1. Spray large saucepan with cooking spray; heat over medium heat until hot. Add carrots, bell pepper, celery, onion and garlic; cook and stir 5 minutes. Add flour and curry powder; cook and stir 1 to 2 minutes.

2. Add chicken broth, milk, chicken, tomato, apple, rice, salt and black pepper; heat to a boil. Reduce heat to low and simmer, covered, 20 minutes or until rice is tender.

*Makes 8 servings*

*Mulligatawny Soup*

# BOUNTY SOUP

### ♥ ♥ ♥

½ pound yellow squash
2 cups frozen mixed vegetables
1 teaspoon dried parsley flakes
⅛ teaspoon dried rosemary
⅛ teaspoon dried thyme leaves
⅛ teaspoon salt
⅛ teaspoon ground black pepper
2 teaspoons vegetable oil
3 boneless skinless chicken breast halves
  (about ¾ pound), diced
1 can (about 14 ounces) fat-free reduced-sodium chicken broth
1 can (14½ ounces) stewed tomatoes, undrained

1. Cut wide part of squash in half lengthwise, lay flat and cut crosswise into ¼-inch slices. Place squash, mixed vegetables, parsley, rosemary, thyme, salt and pepper in medium bowl.

2. Heat oil in large saucepan over medium-high heat. Add chicken; stir-fry 2 minutes. Stir in vegetables and seasonings. Add broth and tomatoes with liquid, breaking large tomatoes apart. Cover; bring to a boil. Reduce heat to low. Cover; cook 5 minutes or until vegetables are tender.

*Makes 4 servings*

**Prep and Cook Time:** 30 minutes

*Bounty Soup*

# BEEFY BROCCOLI & CHEESE SOUP

♥ ♥ ♥

2 cups chicken broth
1 package (10 ounces) frozen chopped broccoli, thawed
¼ cup chopped onion
¼ pound ground beef
1 cup milk
2 tablespoons all-purpose flour
4 ounces (1 cup) shredded sharp Cheddar cheese
½ teaspoon dried oregano leaves
Salt and ground black pepper

Bring broth to a boil in medium saucepan. Add broccoli and onion; cook 5 minutes or until broccoli is tender.

Meanwhile, brown ground beef in small skillet; drain. Gradually add milk to flour, mixing until well blended. Add with ground beef to broth mixture; cook, stirring constantly, until mixture is thickened and bubbly.

Add cheese and oregano; stir until cheese is melted. Season to taste with salt and pepper.                                    *Makes 4 to 5 servings*

*Beefy Broccoli & Cheese Soup*

# SAVORY BEAN STEW

♥ ♥ ♥

1 tablespoon olive or vegetable oil
1 cup frozen vegetable seasoning blend (onions, celery, red and green bell peppers)
1 can (15½ ounces) chick-peas, rinsed and drained
1 can (15 ounces) pinto beans, rinsed and drained
1 can (15 ounces) black beans, rinsed and drained
1 can (14½ ounces) diced tomatoes with roasted garlic, undrained
¾ teaspoon *each* dried thyme leaves and sage leaves
½ to ¾ teaspoon dried oregano leaves
¾ cup vegetable broth or chicken broth, divided
1 tablespoon all-purpose flour
   Salt and ground black pepper
   Polenta (page 38)

Heat oil in large saucepan over medium-heat until hot. Add vegetable seasoning blend; cook and stir 5 minutes. Stir in beans, tomatoes and herbs. Mix ½ cup vegetable broth and flour. Stir into bean mixture; bring to a boil. Boil, stirring constantly, 1 minute. Reduce heat to low; simmer, covered, 10 minutes. Add remaining ¼ cup broth to stew; season to taste with salt and pepper. While stew is simmering, prepare Polenta.

*Makes 6 (1-cup) servings*

**Prep and Cook Time:** 30 minutes

*continued on page 38*

*Savory Bean Stew*

*Savory Bean Stew, continued*

## POLENTA

  **3  cups water**
¾  **cup yellow cornmeal**
¾  **teaspoon salt**
    **Ground white pepper to taste**

Bring 3 cups water to a boil. Reduce heat to medium; gradually stir in cornmeal and salt. Cook 5 to 8 minutes, stirring constantly, or until cornmeal thickens and holds its shape, but is still soft. Season to taste with pepper. Spread Polenta over plate and top with stew.

*Grandma's Secret: The liquid in canned beans contains a large amount of salt. To rid the beans of this excess salt, drain the beans in a colander and rinse them with cold running water.*

# DIJON LAMB STEW

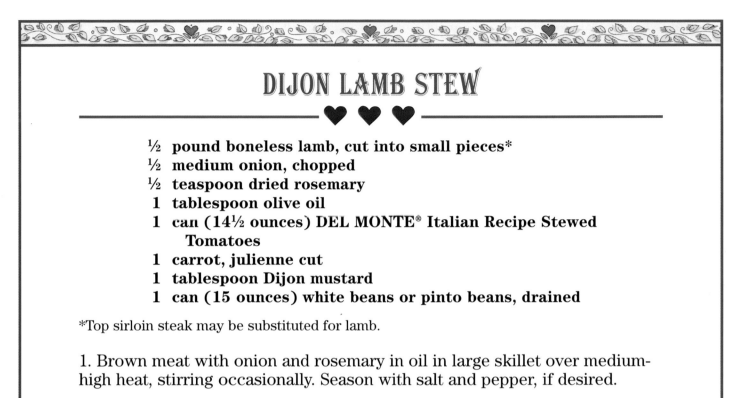

♥ ♥ ♥

½   **pound boneless lamb, cut into small pieces***
½   **medium onion, chopped**
½   **teaspoon dried rosemary**
1   **tablespoon olive oil**
1   **can (14½ ounces) DEL MONTE® Italian Recipe Stewed Tomatoes**
1   **carrot, julienne cut**
1   **tablespoon Dijon mustard**
1   **can (15 ounces) white beans or pinto beans, drained**

*Top sirloin steak may be substituted for lamb.

1. Brown meat with onion and rosemary in oil in large skillet over medium-high heat, stirring occasionally. Season with salt and pepper, if desired.

2. Add tomatoes, carrot and mustard. Cover and cook over medium heat, 10 minutes; add beans.

3. Cook, uncovered, over medium heat 5 minutes, stirring occasionally. Garnish with sliced ripe olives and chopped parsley, if desired.

*Makes 4 servings*

**Prep Time:** 10 minutes
**Cook Time:** 20 minutes

# BRUNSWICK STEW

❤ ❤ ❤

Nonstick cooking spray
12 ounces smoked ham or cooked chicken breast, cut into
    ¾- to 1-inch cubes
1 cup sliced onion
4½ teaspoons all-purpose flour
1 can (14½ ounces) stewed tomatoes, undrained
2 cups frozen mixed vegetables for soup (such as okra,
    lima beans, potatoes, celery, corn, carrots, green
    beans and onions)
1 cup chicken broth
Salt and ground black pepper

1. Spray large saucepan with nonstick cooking spray; heat over medium heat until hot. Add ham and onion; cook 5 minutes or until ham is browned. Stir in flour; cook over medium to medium-low heat 1 minute, stirring constantly.

2. Stir in tomatoes, mixed vegetables and broth; bring to a boil. Reduce heat to low; simmer, covered, 5 to 8 minutes or until vegetables are tender. Simmer, uncovered, 5 to 8 minutes or until slightly thickened. Season to taste with salt and pepper.                    *Makes 4 (1-cup) servings*

**Serving suggestion:** Brunswick Stew is excellent served over rice or squares of cornbread.

**Prep and Cook Time:** 30 minutes

*Brunswick Stew*

# GREEK-STYLE CHICKEN STEW

♥ ♥ ♥

    3  pounds skinless chicken breasts
       All-purpose flour
       Nonstick cooking spray
    2  cups cubed peeled eggplant
    2  cups sliced mushrooms
    ¾  cup coarsely chopped onion (about 1 medium)
    2  cloves garlic, minced
    1  teaspoon dried oregano leaves
    ½  teaspoon *each* dried basil leaves and thyme leaves
    2  cups fat-free reduced-sodium chicken broth
    ¼  cup dry sherry or fat-free low-sodium chicken broth
    ¼  teaspoon *each* salt and ground black pepper
    1  can (14 ounces) artichoke hearts, drained
    3  cups hot cooked wide egg noodles

1. Coat chicken with flour. Spray Dutch oven or large skillet with cooking spray; heat over medium heat until hot. Cook chicken 10 to 15 minutes or until browned on all sides. Remove chicken; drain fat from Dutch oven.

2. Add eggplant, mushrooms, onion, garlic, oregano, basil and thyme to Dutch oven; cook and stir over medium heat 5 minutes. Return chicken to Dutch oven. Stir in chicken broth, sherry, salt and pepper; heat to a boil. Reduce heat to low and simmer, covered, about 1 hour or until chicken is no longer pink in center and juices run clear, adding artichoke hearts during last 20 minutes of cooking. Serve over noodles.     *Makes 6 entrée servings*

*Greek-Style Chicken Stew*

# PORK AND VEGETABLE STEW WITH NOODLES

❤ ❤ ❤

2 tablespoons vegetable oil
1 pound lean boneless pork, cut into ¾-inch cubes
3 cups beef broth
3 tablespoons chopped fresh parsley, divided
1 can (14½ ounces) stewed tomatoes
1 large carrot, sliced
3 green onions, sliced
2 teaspoons Dijon mustard
¼ teaspoon rubbed sage
3 cups uncooked noodles
1 teaspoon butter or margarine
2 tablespoons all-purpose flour
⅓ cup cold water
Apples and parsley for garnish (optional)

Heat oil in large saucepan over medium-high heat. Add meat; brown, stirring frequently. Add beef broth. Stir in 1 tablespoon chopped parsley, tomatoes, carrot, onions, mustard, sage and pepper. Bring to a boil over high heat. Reduce heat to medium-low; simmer, uncovered, 30 minutes.

Meanwhile, cook noodles according to package directions; drain. Add reserved 2 tablespoons chopped parsley and butter; toss lightly. Keep warm until ready to serve.

Stir flour into cold water in cup until smooth. Stir into stew. Cook and stir over medium heat until slightly thickened. Ladle stew over noodles. Garnish, if desired.

*Makes 4 servings*

*Pork and Vegetable Stew with Noodles*

# NAVAJO LAMB STEW WITH CORNMEAL DUMPLINGS

♥ ♥ ♥

2   pounds lean lamb stew meat with bones, cut into 2-inch pieces, *or* 1½ pounds lean boneless lamb, cut into 1½-inch cubes

1   teaspoon salt

½   teaspoon ground black pepper

2   tablespoons plus 1½ teaspoons vegetable oil, divided

1   large onion, chopped

1   clove garlic, minced

4   cups water

2   tablespoons tomato paste

2   teaspoons chili powder

1   teaspoon ground coriander

3   small potatoes, cut into 1½-inch chunks

2   large carrots, cut into 1-inch pieces

1   package (10 ounces) frozen whole kernel corn

⅓   cup coarsely chopped celery leaves

Cornmeal Dumplings (page 48)

1. Sprinkle meat with salt and pepper. Heat 2 tablespoons oil in 5-quart Dutch oven over medium-high heat. Add meat, a few pieces at a time; cook until browned, stirring occasionally. Transfer meat to medium bowl. Heat remaining 1½ teaspoons oil in Dutch oven over medium heat.

*continued on page 48*

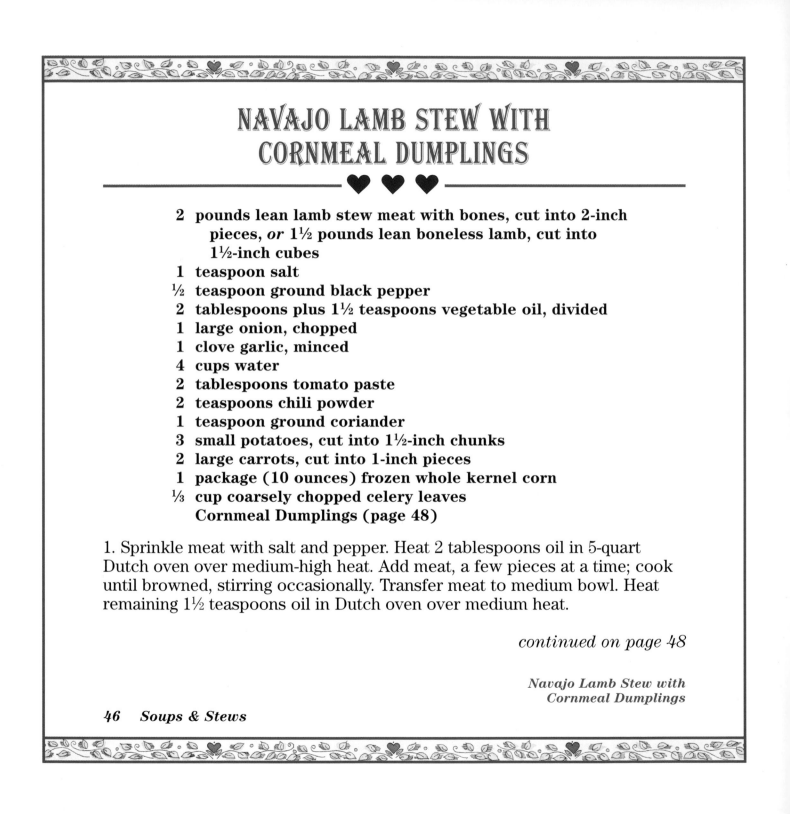

*Navajo Lamb Stew with Cornmeal Dumplings*

*Navajo Lamb Stew with Cornmeal Dumplings, continued*

2. Add onion and garlic; cook and stir until onion is tender. Stir in water, tomato paste, chili powder and coriander. Return meat to Dutch oven. Add potatoes, carrots, corn and chopped celery leaves. Bring to a boil. Cover; reduce heat to low.

3. Simmer 1 hour and 15 minutes or until meat is tender. During last 15 minutes of cooking, prepare Cornmeal Dumplings. Drop dough onto stew to make 6 dumplings. Cover and simmer 18 minutes or until dumplings are firm to the touch and toothpick inserted into centers comes out clean. To serve, spoon stew onto individual plates; serve with dumplings.

*Makes 6 servings*

## CORNMEAL DUMPLINGS

½ **cup yellow cornmeal**
½ **cup all-purpose flour**
1 **teaspoon baking powder**
¼ **teaspoon salt**
2½ **tablespoons cold butter or margarine**
½ **cup milk**

Combine cornmeal, flour, baking powder and salt in medium bowl. Cut in butter with pastry blender or 2 knives until mixture resembles coarse crumbs; make a well in center. Pour in milk all at once; stir with fork until mixture forms dough.

*Makes 6 dumplings*

# STICK-TO-YOUR-RIBS HEARTY BEEF STEW

♥ ♥ ♥

1½ pounds lean beef stew meat, cut into bite-size pieces
¼ cup all-purpose flour
½ teaspoon seasoned salt
⅓ cup WESSON® Vegetable Oil
2 medium onions, cut into 1-inch pieces
1 (14½-ounce) can beef broth
1 (8-ounce) can HUNT'S® Tomato Sauce
4 medium potatoes, peeled and cubed
5 stalks celery, cut into 1-inch pieces
6 carrots, peeled and cut into 1-inch pieces
1½ teaspoons salt
½ teaspoon Italian seasoning
½ teaspoon pepper
1 tablespoon cornstarch plus 2 tablespoons water

In a bag, toss beef with flour and seasoned salt until well coated. In a large Dutch oven, in hot Wesson® Oil, brown beef with onions until tender. Add *remaining* ingredients *except* cornstarch mixture; stir until well blended. Bring to a boil; reduce heat and simmer, covered, for 1 hour 15 minutes or until beef is tender. Stir cornstarch mixture; whisk into stew. Continue to cook an additional 10 minutes, stirring occasionally.

*Makes 6 to 8 servings*

**Tip:** For a fancier stew, reduce beef broth by ½ cup and add ½ cup red wine.

# BISTRO BURGUNDY STEW

❤ ❤ ❤

| | |
|---|---|
| 1 | pound boneless beef sirloin, cut into 1½-inch pieces |
| 3 | tablespoons all-purpose flour |
| 6 | slices bacon, cut into 1-inch pieces (about ¼ pound) |
| 2 | cloves garlic, crushed |
| 3 | carrots, peeled and cut into 1-inch pieces (about 1½ cups) |
| ¾ | cup Burgundy or other dry red wine |
| ½ | cup GREY POUPON® Dijon Mustard |
| ½ | cup beef broth or lower sodium beef broth |
| 12 | small mushrooms |
| 1½ | cups green onions, cut into 1½-inch pieces |
| | Tomato rose and parsley for garnish |
| | Breadsticks, optional |

Coat beef with flour, shaking off excess; set aside.

In large skillet, over medium heat, cook bacon just until done; pour off excess fat. Add beef and garlic; cook until browned. Add carrots, wine, mustard and beef broth. Heat to a boil; reduce heat. Cover; simmer 30 minutes or until carrots are tender, stirring occasionally. Stir in mushrooms and green onions; cook 10 minutes more, stirring occasionally. Garnish with tomato rose and parsley. Serve with breadsticks, if desired.

*Makes 4 servings*

*Bistro Burgundy Stew*

# FAVORITE BEEF STEW

♥ ♥ ♥

1½ pounds beef stew meat, cut into ¾-inch cubes
3 tablespoons all-purpose flour
1 teaspoon salt
½ teaspoon ground black pepper
2 tablespoons vegetable oil
1 cup canned beef broth
1 can (16 ounces) whole tomatoes, cut-up, undrained
1 clove garlic, minced
1 bay leaf
1 tablespoon Worcestershire sauce
½ teaspoon dried thyme leaves
2 potatoes, peeled and cut into ½-inch pieces
1 cup frozen pearl onions
2 carrots, cut into ½-inch pieces
2 ribs celery, cut into ½-inch pieces

1. Place meat in large bowl; sprinkle with flour, salt and pepper. Toss lightly to coat. Heat oil in 5-quart Dutch oven over medium-high heat. Add meat; brown, stirring frequently.

2. Add broth, tomatoes with liquid, garlic, bay leaf, Worcestershire sauce and thyme; bring to a boil over high heat. Reduce heat to low; simmer, uncovered, 1½ hours, stirring occasionally.

3. Increase heat to medium. Add potatoes, onions, carrots and celery; heat until boiling. Reduce heat to low; simmer, uncovered, 30 minutes or until meat and vegetables are tender.                    *Makes 6 servings*

*Favorite Beef Stew*

# Main Dishes

## ROASTED CORNISH HENS WITH DOUBLE MUSHROOM STUFFING

❤ ❤ ❤

2 Cornish hens (about 1½ pounds each)
½ teaspoon salt
¼ teaspoon ground black pepper
3 tablespoons I CAN'T BELIEVE IT'S NOT BUTTER!® SPREAD
1 tablespoon finely chopped shallot or onion
2 teaspoons chopped fresh tarragon leaves or
   ½ teaspoon dried tarragon leaves, crushed (optional)
½ lemon, cut in 2 wedges
1 tablespoon all-purpose flour
   Double Mushroom Stuffing (page 57)

Preheat oven to 425°F. Season hens and hen cavities with salt and pepper.

*continued on page 56*

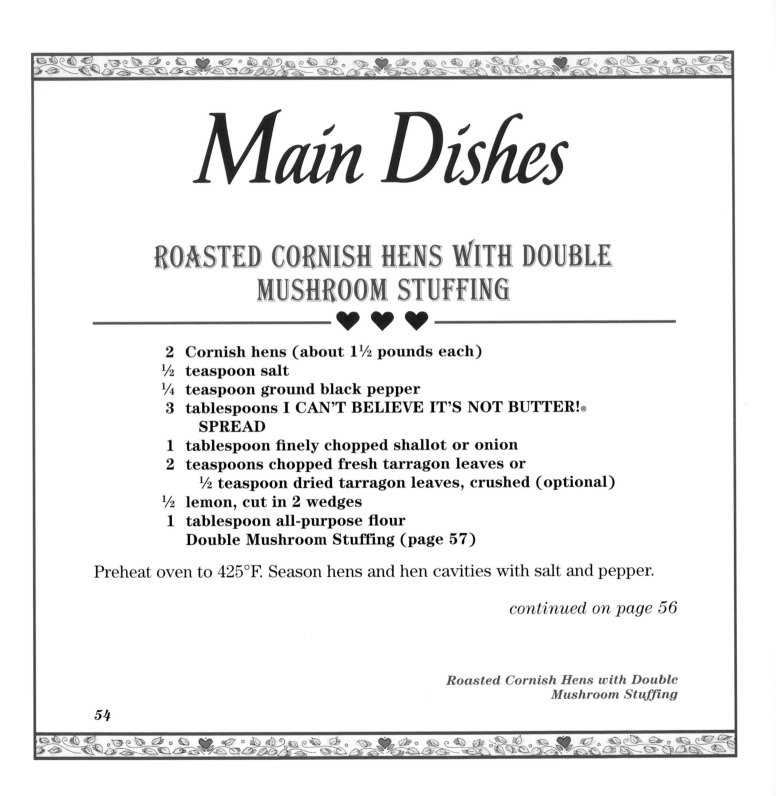

*Roasted Cornish Hens with Double
Mushroom Stuffing*

*Roasted Cornish Hens with Double Mushroom Stuffing, continued*

In small bowl, blend 3 tablespoons I Can't Believe It's Not Butter! Spread, shallot and tarragon. Evenly spread under skin, then place 1 lemon wedge in each hen.

In 18×12-inch roasting pan, on rack, arrange hens breast side up; tie legs together with string. Roast uncovered 15 minutes.

Meanwhile, prepare Double Mushroom Stuffing.

Decrease heat to 350°F. and place Double Mushroom Stuffing casserole in oven with hens. Continue roasting hens 30 minutes or until meat thermometer inserted in thickest part of the thigh reaches 180°F. and stuffing is golden. Remove hens to serving platter and keep warm. Remove rack from pan.

Skim fat from pan drippings.

Blend flour with reserved broth from stuffing; stir into pan drippings. Place roasting pan over heat and bring to a boil over high heat, stirring frequently. Reduce heat to low and simmer, stirring occasionally, 1 minute or until gravy is thickened. Serve gravy and stuffing with hens.     *Makes 2 servings*

*continued on page 57*

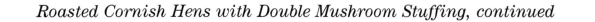

*Roasted Cornish Hens with Double Mushroom Stuffing, continued*

## DOUBLE MUSHROOM STUFFING

3 tablespoons I CAN'T BELIEVE IT'S NOT BUTTER!® SPREAD
½ cup chopped onion
2 cups sliced white and/or shiitake mushrooms
2½ cups fresh ½-inch Italian or French bread cubes
1 can (14½ ounces) chicken broth
2 tablespoons chopped fresh parsley

In 12-inch nonstick skillet, melt I Can't Believe It's Not Butter! Spread over medium-high heat and cook onion, stirring occasionally, 2 minutes or until softened. Add mushrooms and cook, stirring occasionally, 4 minutes or until golden. Stir in bread, ¾ cup broth (reserve remaining broth) and parsley. Season, if desired, with salt and ground black pepper. Spoon into greased 1-quart casserole.

During last 30 minutes of roasting, place stuffing casserole in oven with hens. Cook until stuffing is heated through and golden.

*Makes 2 servings*

# CLASSIC CHICKEN MARSALA

♥ ♥ ♥

- 2 tablespoons unsalted butter
- 1 tablespoon vegetable oil
- 4 boneless skinless chicken breast halves
- 4 slices (1 ounce each) mozzarella cheese
- 12 capers, drained
- 4 flat anchovy fillets, drained
- 1 tablespoon chopped fresh parsley
- 1 clove garlic, minced
- 3 tablespoons Marsala wine
- $\frac{2}{3}$ cup heavy or whipping cream
  Hot cooked pasta (optional)

Heat butter and oil in large skillet over medium-high heat until melted. Add chicken; reduce heat to medium. Cook, uncovered, 5 to 6 minutes per side or until chicken is golden brown. Remove from heat. Top each chicken breast with 1 cheese slice, 3 capers and 1 anchovy fillet.

Return skillet to heat. Sprinkle chicken with parsley. Cover and cook over low heat 3 minutes or until cheese is semi-melted and chicken is no longer pink in center. Remove chicken with slotted spatula to serving dish; keep warm.

Add garlic to drippings remaining in skillet; cook and stir over medium heat 30 seconds. Stir in wine; cook and stir 45 seconds, scraping up any brown bits in skillet. Stir in cream. Cook and stir 3 minutes or until sauce thickens slightly. Spoon sauce over chicken and serve with pasta, if desired.

*Makes 4 servings*

*Classic Chicken Marsala*

# HERBED BUTTER CHICKEN

♥ ♥ ♥

3 tablespoons minced fresh basil
2 teaspoons minced fresh oregano
2 teaspoons minced fresh rosemary
3 tablespoons minced shallots or green onion
2 tablespoons butter, softened
3 cloves garlic, minced
2 teaspoons grated lemon peel
½ teaspoon salt
¼ teaspoon black pepper
4 chicken legs with thighs *or* 1 whole chicken
    (about 3½ pounds), quartered
1 tablespoon olive oil
    Fresh oregano sprigs
    Lemon peel strips

Combine herbs, shallots, butter, garlic, lemon peel, salt and pepper in medium bowl. Loosen chicken skin by gently pushing fingers between the skin and chicken, keeping skin intact. Gently rub herb mixture under skin of chicken, forcing it into the leg section; secure skin with wooden picks. (Soak wooden picks in hot water 15 minutes to prevent burning.) Cover and refrigerate chicken at least ½ hour. Brush chicken with oil. Arrange medium KINGSFORD® Briquets on each side of rectangular metal or foil drip pan. Grill chicken, skin side down, in center of grid on covered grill 20 minutes. Turn chicken and cook 20 to 25 minutes or until juices run clear. Garnish with oregano sprigs and lemon strips. *Makes 4 servings*

*Herbed Butter Chicken*

# ROASTED ROSEMARY-LEMON CHICKEN

❤ ❤ ❤

1 whole chicken (3¼ pounds)
1 lemon, cut into eighths
¼ cup fresh parsley sprigs
4 sprigs fresh rosemary
3 leaves fresh sage
2 sprigs fresh thyme
½ teaspoon ground black pepper
1 can (about 14 ounces) chicken broth
1 cup sliced onion
6 cloves garlic
1 cup thinly sliced carrots
1 cup thinly sliced zucchini

1. Preheat oven to 350°F. Trim fat from chicken. Rinse chicken and pat dry with paper towels. Fill cavity of chicken with lemon, parsley, rosemary, sage, thyme and pepper. Close cavity with skewers.

2. Combine chicken broth, onion and garlic in heavy roasting pan. Place chicken in broth mixture. Roast chicken, basting occasionally with broth mixture, 1½ hours or until internal temperature reaches 180°F when tested with meat thermometer inserted into thickest part of thigh not touching any bone. Remove chicken to serving platter.

3. Combine carrots and zucchini in small saucepan with tight-fitting lid. Add ¼ cup water; bring to a boil over high heat. Reduce heat to medium. Cover and steam 4 minutes or until vegetables are crisp-tender. Drain.

4. Remove skewers from chicken. Discard lemon and herbs from cavity of chicken. Cut chicken into pieces. Remove onion and garlic from pan with slotted spoon to medium serving bowl or plate. Add carrots and zucchini; mix well. Arrange vegetable mixture around chicken.     *Makes 6 servings*

# MUSTARD CHICKEN
❤ ❤ ❤

1 **large *or* 2 small broiling chickens, cut into serving**
   **pieces and skinned**
   **Freshly ground black pepper**
½ **cup prepared mustard***
2 **tablespoons brown sugar**
1 **clove garlic, minced**
½ **teaspoon dry mustard**
   **Dry bread crumbs**

*May substitute ¼ cup prepared mustard and ¼ cup Dijon mustard

Preheat oven to 400°F. Sprinkle chicken pieces with pepper; place on rack in roasting pan and bake until lightly golden, 10 to 15 minutes.

Combine prepared mustard, sugar, garlic and dry mustard; blend well. Brush both sides of chicken pieces with mustard mixture. Roll in bread crumbs, coating lightly. Return to rack and bake 20 minutes. Turn pieces over and bake another 30 minutes, or until chicken is tender and coating is crusty.
*Makes 4 to 6 servings*

*Favorite recipe from **The Sugar Association, Inc.***

# YANKEE POT ROAST AND VEGETABLES

### ♥ ♥ ♥

1 beef chuck pot roast (2½ pounds)
   Salt and ground black pepper
3 medium (about 1 pound) baking potatoes, unpeeled
   and cut into quarters
2 large carrots, cut into ¾-inch slices
2 ribs celery, cut into ¾-inch slices
1 medium onion, sliced
1 large parsnip, peeled and cut into ¾-inch slices
2 bay leaves
1 teaspoon dried rosemary leaves
½ teaspoon dried thyme leaves
½ cup reduced-sodium beef broth

## SLOW COOKER DIRECTIONS

Trim excess fat from meat and discard. Cut into serving pieces; sprinkle with salt and pepper. Combine vegetables, bay leaves, rosemary and thyme in slow cooker. Place beef over vegetables. Pour broth over beef. Cover and cook on LOW 8½ to 9 hours or until beef is fork-tender. Remove beef to serving platter. Arrange vegetables around beef. Remove and discard bay leaves.

*Makes 10 to 12 servings*

*Yankee Pot Roast and Vegetables*

# PEPPERED BEEF RIB ROAST

❤ ❤ ❤

  1½   tablespoons black peppercorns
  ¼   cup Dijon mustard
  2   cloves garlic, minced
  1   boneless beef rib roast (2½ to 3 pounds), well trimmed
       Sour Cream Sauce (page 68)

Place peppercorns in small resealable plastic food storage bag. Squeeze out excess air; close bag securely. Pound peppercorns using flat side of meat mallet or rolling pin until cracked. Set aside.

Combine mustard and garlic in small bowl; spread over top and sides of roast. Sprinkle pepper over mustard mixture.

Place roast, pepper-side up, on grid directly over drip pan. Grill, covered, over medium heat 1 hour to 1 hour 10 minutes for medium or until internal temperature reaches 145°F when tested with meat thermometer inserted into the thickest part of roast. Add 4 to 9 briquettes to both sides of the fire after 45 minutes to maintain medium heat.

*continued on page 68*

*Peppered Beef Rib Roast*

*Peppered Beef Rib Roast, continued*

Meanwhile, prepare Sour Cream Sauce. Cover; refrigerate until serving.

Transfer roast to cutting board; cover with foil. Let stand 10 to 15 minutes before carving. Internal tmeperature will continue to rise 5°F to 10°F during stand time. Serve with Sour Cream Sauce.          *Makes 6 to 8 servings*

## SOUR CREAM SAUCE

  ¾  **cup sour cream**
  2  **tablespoons prepared horseradish**
  1  **tablespoon balsamic vinegar**
  ½  **teaspoon sugar**

Combine all ingredients in small bowl; mix well.          *Makes about 1 cup*

# STUFFED SALISBURY STEAK WITH MUSHROOM & ONION TOPPING

♥ ♥ ♥

2 pounds ground beef
¼ cup FRENCH'S® Worcestershire Sauce
2⅔ cups FRENCH'S® French Fried Onions, divided
1 teaspoon garlic salt
½ teaspoon ground black pepper
4 ounces Cheddar cheese, cut into 6 sticks (about
    2×½×½ inches)
Mushroom Topping (recipe follows)

Combine beef, Worcestershire, *1⅓ cups* French Fried Onions, garlic salt and pepper. Divide meat evenly into 6 portions. Place 1 stick cheese in center of each portion, firmly pressing and shaping meat into ovals around cheese.

Place steaks on grid. Grill over medium-high coals 15 minutes or until meat thermometer inserted into beef reaches 160°F, turning once. Serve with Mushroom Topping and sprinkle with remaining *1⅓ cups* onions.

*Makes 6 servings*

## MUSHROOM TOPPING

2 tablespoons butter or margarine
1 package (12 ounces) mushrooms, quartered
2 tablespoons FRENCH'S® Worcestershire Sauce

Melt butter in large skillet over medium-high heat. Add mushrooms; cook 5 minutes or until browned, stirring often. Add Worcestershire. Reduce heat to low. Cook 5 minutes, stirring occasionally. *Makes 6 servings*

# BRISKET OF BEEF

♥ ♥ ♥

1 whole well-trimmed beef brisket (about 5 pounds)
4 cloves garlic, minced
½ teaspoon ground black pepper
2 large onions, cut into ¼-inch slices and separated into rings
1 bottle (12 ounces) chili sauce
¾ cup beef broth, beer or water
2 tablespoons Worcestershire sauce
1 tablespoon packed brown sugar

Preheat oven to 350°F. Place brisket, fat side up, in shallow roasting pan. Spread garlic evenly over brisket; sprinkle with pepper. Arrange onions over brisket. Combine chili sauce, broth, Worcestershire sauce and sugar; pour over brisket and onions. Cover with heavy-duty foil or roasting pan lid.

Roast 2 hours. Turn brisket over; stir onions into sauce and spoon over brisket. Cover; roast 1 to 2 hours more or until fork-tender. Transfer brisket to cutting board. Tent with foil; let stand 10 minutes.

Stir juices in roasting pan. Spoon off and discard fat from juices. (Juices may be thinned to desired consistency with water or thickened by simmering, uncovered, in saucepan.) Carve brisket across grain into thin slices. Spoon juices over brisket. *Makes 10 to 12 servings*

*Brisket of Beef*

# LEMONY BEEF, VEGETABLES & BARLEY

♥ ♥ ♥

1  pound lean ground beef
8  ounces mushrooms, sliced
1  medium onion, chopped
1  clove garlic, crushed
1  can (about 14 ounces) beef broth
½  cup quick-cooking barley
½  teaspoon salt
¼  teaspoon pepper
1  package (10 ounces) frozen peas and carrots,
    defrosted
1  teaspoon grated lemon peel

1. In large nonstick skillet, cook and stir ground beef, mushrooms, onion and garlic over medium heat 8 to 10 minutes or until beef is no longer pink, breaking beef up into ¾-inch crumbles. Pour off drippings.

2. Stir in broth, barley, salt and pepper. Bring to a boil; reduce heat to medium-low. Cover tightly; simmer 10 minutes.

3. Add peas and carrots; continue cooking 2 to 5 minutes or until barley is tender. Stir in lemon peel.                    *Makes 4 (1½-cup) servings*

**Prep & Cook Time:** 30 minutes

*Favorite recipe from **National Cattlemen's Beef Association***

*Lemony Beef, Vegetables & Barley*

# RIB EYE ROAST AND OVEN BROWNED VEGETABLES WITH EASY SAVORY SAUCE

♥ ♥ ♥

1 (4-pound) boneless beef rib eye roast (small end)
2 tablespoons minced fresh rosemary leaves *or*
   2 teaspoons dried rosemary leaves, crushed
4 cloves garlic, crushed
1 teaspoon each dry mustard, salt and black pepper
2 tablespoons vegetable oil
3 medium baking potatoes (about 1 pound), peeled,
   quartered
4 small onions (about ¾ pound), peeled, cut in half
2 large sweet potatoes (about 1 pound), peeled, halved
   and cut into quarters
   Easy Savory Sauce (recipe follows)

Combine rosemary, garlic, mustard, salt and pepper. Rub half of herb mixture evenly over surface of beef roast. Add oil to remaining herb mixture. Place vegetables in large bowl; add herb-oil mixture, tossing to coat evenly. Place roast, fat side up, on rack in shallow roasting pan. Insert meat thermometer so bulb is centered in thickest part of roast but not resting in fat. Arrange coated vegetables around roast. Do not add water. Do not cover. Roast in 350°F oven to desired degree of doneness. For roast, allow 20 to 22 minutes per pound for rare or medium. Remove roast when meat thermometer registers 135°F for rare; 155°F for medium.

Cook vegetables 1½ hours or until tender. Place roast on carving board; return vegetables to oven if longer cooking is necessary. Tent roast with foil and let stand 15 minutes before carving. Roast should continue to rise about 5°F in temperature to 140°F for rare; 160°F for medium. Meanwhile, prepare Easy Savory Sauce. Carve roast into slices. Serve with vegetables and sauce.

*Makes 8 servings*

**Note:** A boneless beef rib eye roast will yield three 3-ounce cooked servings per pound.

## EASY SAVORY SAUCE

|   |   |
|---|---|
| 1½ | teaspoons dry mustard |
| 1 | teaspoon water |
| 1 | jar (12 ounces) prepared brown gravy* |
| ¼ | cup currant jelly |

*One can (13¾ ounces) ready-to-serve beef broth may be substituted for prepared brown gravy. In small saucepan, combine beef broth and 2 tablespoons cornstarch, mixing well. Cook over medium-high heat 3 minutes or until slightly thickened, stirring occasionally. Use as directed for sauce.

Combine mustard and water in small saucepan, stirring to dissolve mustard. Stir in brown gravy and currant jelly. Cook over medium heat about 5 minutes or until mixture is bubbly and jelly is melted, stirring occasionally.

*Makes 2 cups*

*Favorite recipe from* **National Cattlemen's Beef Association**

# HERBED ROAST

♥ ♥ ♥

        1   beef top round roast (about 3 pounds)
      ⅓   cup Dijon-style mustard
    1½   teaspoons dried thyme, crushed
        1   teaspoon dried rosemary, crushed
        1   teaspoon LAWRY'S® Seasoned Pepper
        1   teaspoon LAWRY'S® Garlic Powder with Parsley
      ½   teaspoon LAWRY'S® Seasoned Salt

Brush all sides of roast with mustard. In small bowl, combine remaining ingredients; mix well. Sprinkle on top and sides of roast, pressing into meat. Place roast, fat side up, on rack in roasting pan. Roast in 325°F oven, 50 minutes to 1 hour or until internal temperature reaches 160°F. Remove roast from oven. Let stand, covered, 15 minutes.          *Makes 6 to 8 servings*

**Serving Suggestion:** Slice thinly and serve with roasted potato wedges and steamed vegetables.

*Herbed Roast*

# ITALIAN MEAT LOAF PATTIES

❤ ❤ ❤

2 packages (12 ounces each) extra wide noodles
2 tablespoons butter or margarine, melted
1 can (15 ounces) DEL MONTE® Original Sloppy Joe
  Sauce
2 pounds ground beef or turkey
1 cup dry bread crumbs
2 eggs, beaten
1 tablespoon dried minced onions

1. Preheat oven to 375°F.

2. Cook noodles according to package directions; drain. Toss with butter; keep hot.

3. Set aside half of sauce to brush on patties. In large bowl, combine remaining sauce with remaining ingredients; mix with fork. On large, greased baking sheet, shape meat mixture into 8 (1-inch-thick) oblong patties. Brush reserved sauce over patties.

4. Bake 20 minutes or until no longer pink in center. Serve patties with hot, buttered noodles. Garnish, if desired.           *Makes 8 servings*

**Prep Time:** 5 minutes
**Cook Time:** 20 minutes

*Italian Meat Loaf Patties*

# PEPPERED BEEF TIP ROAST WITH CORN PUDDING

❤ ❤ ❤

1 (3½- to 5-pound) beef tip roast
2 teaspoons *each:* cracked black pepper and dry mustard
½ teaspoon *each:* ground allspice and ground red pepper
1 large clove garlic, minced
1 teaspoon vegetable oil
  Corn Pudding (page 82)

Preheat oven to 325°F.

Combine black pepper, mustard, allspice, ground red pepper and garlic; stir in oil to form paste.

Spread mixture evenly on surface of beef tip roast. Place roast, fat side up, on rack in open roasting pan. Insert meat thermometer so bulb is centered in thickest part of roast. Do not add water. Do not cover. Roast to desired doneness, allowing 30 to 35 minutes per pound. Meanwhile, prepare Corn Pudding.

Remove roast when meat thermometer registers 155°F for medium. Allow roast to stand 15 to 20 minutes in a warm place before carving. Roast will continue to rise about 5°F in temperature to reach 160°F. Serve carved roast with Corn Pudding. *Makes 2 to 4 servings per pound*

*continued on page 82*

*Peppered Beef Tip Roast
with Corn Pudding*

## CORN PUDDING

1  **bag (20 ounces) frozen whole kernel corn, thawed**
1  **small onion, quartered**
2  **cups milk**
2  **eggs, beaten**
1  **package (8½ ounces) corn muffin mix**
½  **teaspoon salt**
1  **cup shredded Cheddar cheese**
1  **cup thinly sliced romaine lettuce**
½  **cup julienned radishes**

Preheat oven to 325°F. Combine corn and onion in food processor; cover and process using on/off pulse until corn is broken but not puréed, scraping side of bowl as necessary. Add milk and eggs; pulse until just blended. Add muffin mix and salt; pulse only until mixed. Pour mixture into greased 11¾×7½-inch baking dish. Bake 45 to 50 minutes or until outside crust is golden brown. Sprinkle pudding with cheese; place under broiler 3 to 4 inches from heat. Broil until cheese is melted and top is crusty. To serve, top with romain lettuce and radishes. *Makes 8 to 10 servings*

*Favorite recipe from* **National Cattlemen's Beef Association**

# ROAST BEEF AND PASTA SALAD

❤ ❤ ❤

9 ounces uncooked radiatore pasta
6 ounces lean roast beef
1 can (15 ounces) kidney beans, rinsed and drained
1 can (15 ounces) whole baby corn, rinsed and drained
1 can (10 ounces) diced tomatoes and green chilies
1 cup cherry tomato halves
½ cup sliced black olives (optional)
2 tablespoons minced fresh parsley
1 tablespoon minced fresh oregano
¼ cup olive oil

1. Cook pasta according to package directions, omitting salt; drain. Rinse in cold water; drain.

2. Slice beef into thin strips. Combine pasta, beef and remaining ingredients in large bowl. Toss to coat. Garnish with fresh oregano, if desired.

*Makes 6 servings*

**Ready to serve in:** 25 minutes

# BEEF STROGANOFF AND ZUCCHINI TOPPED POTATOES

♥ ♥ ♥

4 (8 ounces each) baking potatoes
¾ pound ground beef round
¾ cup chopped onion
1 cup sliced mushrooms
1 beef bouillon cube
2 tablespoons ketchup
1 teaspoon Worcestershire sauce
¼ teaspoon ground black pepper
¼ teaspoon hot pepper sauce
1 medium zucchini, cut into julienned strips
½ cup low-fat sour cream, divided

1. Pierce potatoes in several places with fork. Place in microwave oven on paper towel. Microwave potatoes at HIGH 15 minutes or until softened. Wrap in paper towels. Let stand 5 minutes.

2. Heat large nonstick skillet over medium-high heat until hot. Add beef and onion. Cook and stir 5 minutes or until beef is browned. Add all remaining ingredients except zucchini and sour cream. Cover and simmer 5 minutes. Add zucchini. Cover and cook 3 minutes. Remove from heat. Stir in ¼ cup sour cream. Cover and let stand 5 minutes.

3. Cut potatoes open. Divide beef mixture evenly among potatoes. Top with remaining ¼ cup sour cream. *Makes 4 servings*

*Beef Stroganoff and Zucchini Topped Potatoes*

# MAPLE-GLAZED TURKEY BREAST

♥ ♥ ♥

1 **bone-in turkey breast (5 to 6 pounds)**
**Roast rack (optional)**
¼ **cup pure maple syrup**
2 **tablespoons butter or margarine, melted**
1 **tablespoon bourbon (optional)**
2 **teaspoons freshly grated orange peel**

1. Prepare barbecue grill with rectangular foil drip pan. Bank briquettes on either side of drip pan for indirect cooking.

2. Insert meat thermometer into center of thickest part of turkey breast, not touching bone. Place turkey, bone side down, on roast rack or directly on grid, directly over drip pan. Grill turkey, on covered grill, over medium coals 55 minutes, adding 4 to 9 briquettes to both sides of fire after 45 minutes to maintain medium coals.

3. Combine maple syrup, butter, bourbon and orange peel in small bowl; brush half of mixture over turkey. Continue to grill, covered, 10 minutes. Brush with remaining mixture; continue to grill, covered, about 10 minutes or until internal temperature reaches 170°F when tested with meat thermometer inserted into the thickest part of breast, not touching any bone.

4. Transfer turkey to carving board; let stand 10 to 15 minutes before carving. Internal temperature will continue to rise 5°F to 10°F during stand time. Cut turkey into thin slices. *Makes 6 to 8 servings*

*Maple-Glazed Turkey Breast*

# ROAST TURKEY WITH CRANBERRY STUFFING

♥ ♥ ♥

1 loaf (12 ounces) Italian or French bread, cut into
    ½-inch cubes
2 tablespoons butter
1½ cups chopped onions
1½ cups chopped celery
2 teaspoons poultry seasoning
1 teaspoon dried thyme leaves
½ teaspoon dried rosemary leaves
¼ teaspoon salt
¼ teaspoon ground black pepper
1 cup coarsely chopped fresh cranberries
1 tablespoon sugar
¾ cup fat-free reduced-sodium chicken broth
1 turkey (8 to 10 pounds)

1. Preheat oven to 375°F. Arrange bread on two 15×10-inch jelly roll pans. Bake 12 minutes or until lightly toasted. *Reduce oven temperature to 350°F.*

2. Melt butter in large saucepan over medium heat. Add onions and celery; cook and stir 8 minutes or until vegetables are tender; remove from heat. Add bread cubes, poultry seasoning, thyme, rosemary, salt and pepper; mix well. Combine cranberries and sugar in small bowl; mix well. Add to bread mixture; toss well. Drizzle chicken broth evenly over mixture; toss well.

*continued on page 90*

*Roast Turkey with Cranberry Stuffing*

*Roast Turkey with Cranberry Stuffing, continued*

3. Remove giblets from turkey. Rinse turkey and cavity in cold water; pat dry with paper towels. Fill turkey cavity loosely with stuffing. Place remaining stuffing in casserole sprayed with nonstick cooking spray. Cover casserole; refrigerate until baking time.

4. Spray roasting pan with nonstick cooking spray. Place turkey, breast side up, on rack in roasting pan. Bake 3 hours or until meat thermometer inserted in thickest part of thigh, not touching bone, registers 180°F and juices run clear.

5. Transfer turkey to serving platter. Cover loosely with foil; let stand 10 to 15 minutes. Internal temperature will continue to rise 5°F to 10°F during stand time. Place covered casserole of stuffing in oven; increase temperature to 375°F. Bake 25 to 30 minutes or until hot.

6. Slice turkey and serve with cranberry stuffing. Garnish with fresh rosemary sprigs, if desired.                                          *Makes 10 servings*

*Grandma's Secret*: When you are short on time, use a blender or food processor to chop fresh cranberries. Just a few on and off pulses are enough to get the job done fast.

# ROAST TURKEY WITH HONEY CRANBERRY RELISH

♥ ♥ ♥

1   medium orange
12  ounces fresh or frozen whole cranberries
¾   cup honey
2   pounds sliced roasted turkey breast

Quarter and slice unpeeled orange, removing seeds. Coarsely chop orange and cranberries. Place in medium saucepan and stir in honey. Bring to a boil over medium-high heat. Cook 3 to 4 minutes; cool. Serve over turkey.

*Makes 8 servings*

*Favorite recipe from* **National Honey Board**

*Grandma's Secret: This quick and easy turkey recipe would make a delicious weekday dinner. It is also a tasty way to use up leftover holiday turkey.*

# MINI TURKEY LOAVES

♥ ♥ ♥

1 pound ground turkey
1 small apple, chopped
½ small onion, chopped
½ cup uncooked rolled oats
2 teaspoons Dijon-style mustard
1 teaspoon dried rosemary leaves
1 teaspoon salt
  Dash of ground black pepper
  Cranberry sauce
  Vegetable Stir-Fry (page 94)
  Mashed potatoes (optional)

Preheat oven to 425°F. Grease 12 (2½-inch) muffin cups. Combine turkey, apple, onion, oats, mustard, rosemary, salt and pepper in large bowl. Press into prepared muffin cups. Bake 20 minutes or until lightly browned and no longer pink in center. Top with cranberry sauce. Garnish as desired. Serve with Vegetable Stir-Fry and mashed potatoes, if desired.

*Makes 4 servings*

*continued on page 94*

*Mini Turkey Loaves*

*Mini Turkey Loaves, continued*

## VEGETABLE STIR-FRY

- 1 tablespoon vegetable oil
- 3 to 4 carrots, diagonally sliced
- 2 zucchini, diagonally sliced
- 3 tablespoons orange juice
    Salt and ground black pepper

Heat oil in medium skillet or wok over medium heat. Add carrots; stir-fry 3 minutes. Add zucchini and orange juice; stir-fry 4 minutes or until vegetables are crisp-tender. Season with salt and pepper to taste.

*Grandma's Secret: Ground turkey is usually a combination of light and dark meat. For leaner ground turkey, ask your butcher to grind only the light breast meat, as the darker leg and thigh meat has a higher fat content.*

# TURKEY TETRAZZINI WITH ROASTED RED PEPPERS

❤ ❤ ❤

6 ounces uncooked egg noodles
3 tablespoons butter or margarine
¼ cup all-purpose flour
1 can (about 14 ounces) chicken broth
1 cup whipping cream
2 tablespoons dry sherry
2 cans (6 ounces each) sliced mushrooms, drained
1 jar (7½ ounces) roasted red peppers, cut into strips
2 cups chopped cooked turkey
1 teaspoon dried Italian seasoning
½ cup grated Parmesan cheese

1. Cook egg noodles according to package directions. Drain well. While noodles are cooking, melt butter in medium saucepan over medium heat. Add flour and whisk until smooth. Add chicken broth; bring to a boil over high heat. Remove from heat. Gradually add whipping cream and sherry; stir to combine.

2. Combine mushrooms, peppers and noodles in large bowl; toss to combine. Add half the chicken broth mixture to noodle mixture. Combine remaining chicken broth mixture, turkey and Italian seasoning in large bowl. Spoon noodle mixture into serving dish. Make a well in center of noodles and spoon in turkey mixture. Sprinkle cheese over top.     *Makes 6 servings*

# THREE-CITRUS TURKEY TENDERLOINS

♥ ♥ ♥

- ⅔ cup fresh orange juice, divided
- 3 tablespoons minced shallots or onion
- ½ teaspoon grated lemon peel
- ½ teaspoon grated lime peel
- 2 tablespoons fresh lemon juice
- 2 tablespoons fresh lime juice
- 2 whole turkey tenderloins (about ¾ pound each)
- 1 tablespoon olive oil
- ½ teaspoon salt
- 2½ tablespoons honey
- 1 teaspoon cornstarch

1. Combine ⅓ cup orange juice, shallots, lemon peel, lime peel, lemon juice and lime juice in small bowl; mix well. Reserve ⅓ cup of juice mixture; cover and refrigerate. Place turkey in large resealable plastic food storage bag; add remaining juice mixture to bag. Seal bag tightly, turning to coat. Marinate in refrigerator 1 to 2 hours, turning once.

2. Prepare grill for direct cooking.

3. Drain turkey; discard marinade from bag. Brush turkey with oil; sprinkle with salt. Place turkey on grid. Grill turkey, on covered grill, over medium-hot coals 15 to 20 minutes or until no longer pink in center, turning halfway through grilling time. (If desired, insert instant-read thermometer* into center of thickest part of tenderloin. Thermometer should register 170°F.)

*Continued on page 98*

*Three-Citrus Turkey Tenderloins*

*Three-Citrus Turkey Tenderloins, continued*

4. Meanwhile, combine reserved juice mixture and honey in small saucepan. Combine remaining ⅓ cup orange juice and cornstarch in small bowl; mix until smooth. Add to juice mixture in saucepan. Simmer, uncovered, over medium heat about 5 minutes or until thickened and reduced to ½ cup.

5. Transfer turkey to carving board. Carve turkey crosswise into thin slices; drizzle with sauce. *Makes 4 to 6 servings*

*Do not leave instant-read thermometer in tenderloins during grilling since the thermometer is not heatproof.

*Grandma's Secret: Like beef and pork tenderloins, the tenderloin of the turkey is the leanest cut. Rubbing the tenderloin with oil prior to grilling will seal in juices and help keep the turkey moist.*

# GRAPE AND LAMB STIR-FRY

♥ ♥ ♥

1¼ pounds lamb or beef, cut into thin strips
2 tablespoons cornstarch, divided
2 tablespoons soy sauce, divided
1 clove garlic, minced
1 teaspoon grated fresh ginger
1 cup *each* sliced celery and onion
½ cup chopped green bell pepper
2 tablespoons vegetable oil, divided
2 cups California seedless grapes
¼ cup water
2 tablespoons ketchup
½ teaspoon sugar
¼ teaspoon Worcestershire sauce
Pan-fried noodles or rice

Combine lamb, 1 tablespoon *each* cornstarch and soy sauce, garlic and ginger in large bowl; set aside. In large skillet, stir-fry celery, onion and pepper in 1 tablespoon oil for 1 minute. Add grapes and stir-fry 1 minute longer; remove from pan. Heat remaining 1 tablespoon oil over high heat. Cook and stir lamb about 2 minutes or until browned and cooked to desired degree of doneness. Combine water, ketchup, remaining 1 tablespoon *each* cornstarch and soy sauce, sugar and Worcestershire sauce. Stir into lamb in skillet. Cook until mixture bubbles. Add grape mixture; toss lightly to coat. Heat thoroughly. Serve over pan-fried noodles.          *Makes about 6 servings*

*Favorite recipe from* **California Table Grape Commission**

# LEG OF LAMB WITH WINE MARINADE

❤ ❤ ❤

1½ cups red wine
1 onion, chopped
1 carrot, chopped
1 rib celery, chopped
2 tablespoons chopped fresh parsley
2 tablespoons olive oil
3 cloves garlic, minced
1 tablespoon dried thyme leaves
1 teaspoon salt
1 teaspoon ground black pepper
1½ pounds boneless leg of lamb, trimmed

Combine all ingredients, except lamb, in medium bowl. Place lamb in large resealable plastic food storage bag. Add wine mixture to bag. Close bag securely, turning to coat. Marinate in refrigerator 2 hours or overnight.

Prepare grill for indirect cooking. Drain lamb; reserve marinade.

Place lamb on grid directly over drip pan. Grill, covered, over medium heat about 45 minutes for medium or until internal temperature reaches 145°F when tested with meat thermometer inserted into the thickest part of roast, not touching bone. Brush occasionally with reserved marinade. (Do not brush with marinade during last 5 minutes of grilling.)

Transfer roast to cutting board; let stand 10 to 15 minutes berfore carving. Internal temperature will continue to rise 5°F to 10°F during stand time.

*Makes 4 servings*

*Leg of Lamb with Wine Marinade*

# One-Dish Wonders

## SAVORY CHICKEN AND BISCUITS

♥ ♥ ♥

1 pound boneless skinless chicken thighs or breasts, cut
   into 1-inch pieces
1 medium potato, cut into 1-inch pieces
1 medium yellow onion, cut into 1-inch pieces
8 ounces fresh mushrooms, quartered
1 cup fresh baby carrots
1 cup chopped celery
1 (14½-ounce) can chicken broth
3 cloves garlic, minced
1 teaspoon dried rosemary leaves
1 teaspoon salt
1 teaspoon black pepper
3 tablespoons cornstarch blended with ½ cup cold water
1 cup frozen peas, thawed
1 (4-ounce) jar sliced pimentos, drained
1 package BOB EVANS® Frozen Buttermilk Biscuit Dough

*continued on page 104*

*Savory Chicken and Biscuits*

*Savory Chicken and Bisquits, continued*

Preheat oven to 375°F. Combine chicken, potato, onion, mushrooms, carrots, celery, broth, garlic, rosemary, salt and pepper in large saucepan. Bring to a boil over high heat. Reduce heat to low and simmer, uncovered, 5 minutes. Stir in cornstarch mixture; cook 2 minutes. Stir in peas and pimentos; return to a boil. Transfer chicken mixture to 2-quart casserole dish; arrange frozen biscuits on top. Bake 30 to 35 minutes or until biscuits are golden brown. Refrigerate leftovers.          *Makes 4 to 6 servings*

*Grandma's Secret: Pimentos are small heart-shaped sweet red peppers. The flesh of pimentos is sweeter and more aromatic than that of red bell peppers. They can be found fresh in specialty markets during the summer months. Bottled or canned pimentos are available throughout the year in most supermarkets.*

# PICADILLO CHICKEN

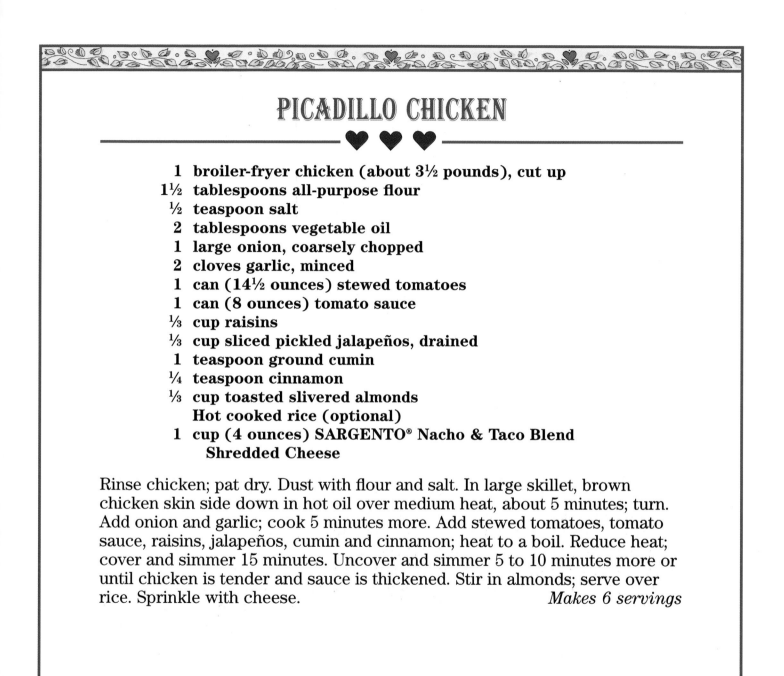

1   broiler-fryer chicken (about 3½ pounds), cut up
1½  tablespoons all-purpose flour
½   teaspoon salt
2   tablespoons vegetable oil
1   large onion, coarsely chopped
2   cloves garlic, minced
1   can (14½ ounces) stewed tomatoes
1   can (8 ounces) tomato sauce
⅓   cup raisins
⅓   cup sliced pickled jalapeños, drained
1   teaspoon ground cumin
¼   teaspoon cinnamon
⅓   cup toasted slivered almonds
    Hot cooked rice (optional)
1   cup (4 ounces) SARGENTO® Nacho & Taco Blend
    Shredded Cheese

Rinse chicken; pat dry. Dust with flour and salt. In large skillet, brown chicken skin side down in hot oil over medium heat, about 5 minutes; turn. Add onion and garlic; cook 5 minutes more. Add stewed tomatoes, tomato sauce, raisins, jalapeños, cumin and cinnamon; heat to a boil. Reduce heat; cover and simmer 15 minutes. Uncover and simmer 5 to 10 minutes more or until chicken is tender and sauce is thickened. Stir in almonds; serve over rice. Sprinkle with cheese.                    *Makes 6 servings*

# CHICKEN BOURGUIGNONNE

♥ ♥ ♥

4 pounds skinless chicken thighs and breasts
  All-purpose flour
  Nonstick cooking spray
2 cups fat-free, reduced-sodium chicken broth
2 cups dry white wine or chicken broth
1 pound whole baby carrots
¼ cup tomato paste
4 cloves garlic, minced
½ teaspoon dried thyme leaves
2 bay leaves
¼ teaspoon *each* salt and ground black pepper
8 ounces fresh or thawed frozen pearl onions
8 ounces whole medium mushrooms
2 cups *each* hot cooked white rice and wild rice
¼ cup minced fresh parsley

Preheat oven to 325°F. Coat chicken with flour. Spray ovenproof Dutch oven or large ovenproof skillet with cooking spray; heat over medium heat until hot. Cook chicken 10 to 15 minutes or until browned on all sides. Drain fat.

Add chicken broth, wine, carrots, tomato paste, garlic, thyme, bay leaves, salt and pepper to Dutch oven; heat to a boil. Cover; transfer to oven. Bake 1 hour. Add onions and mushrooms. Uncover; bake about 35 minutes or until vegetables are tender, and chicken is no longer pink in center and juices run clear. Remove bay leaves. Combine white and wild rice; serve with chicken. Sprinkle with parsley.          *Makes 8 servings*

*Chicken Bourguignonne*

# CHICKEN SKILLET SUPPER

♥ ♥ ♥

1 teaspoon salt
¼ teaspoon ground black pepper
¼ teaspoon ground paprika
⅛ teaspoon garlic powder
1 cut-up whole chicken (about 3 pounds)
1 tablespoon vegetable oil
2 tablespoons water
1 medium onion, chopped
1 medium potato, peeled and cut into 2¼-inch strips
1 can (8 ounces) tomato sauce
1 cup chicken broth
1 teaspoon sugar
1 package (10 ounces) frozen mixed vegetables

Mix salt, pepper, paprika and garlic powder in small bowl; rub over chicken. Heat oil in large skillet over medium heat; add chicken, skin-side down. Cover and cook 10 minutes. Add water to chicken; cover and cook 30 minutes or until chicken is no longer pink and juices run clear, turning chicken over every 10 minutes. Remove chicken from skillet; set aside.

Add onion and potato to pan juices; cook until onion is tender, about 3 minutes. Add tomato sauce, broth and sugar; cook until liquid comes to a boil. Add vegetables and chicken pieces; cover and cook until vegetables are tender, about 10 minutes. Serve hot. *Makes 4 to 6 servings*

*Chicken Skillet Supper*

# CHICKEN MARSALA

❤ ❤ ❤

4 cups (6 ounces) uncooked broad egg noodles
½ cup Italian-style dry bread crumbs
1 teaspoon dried basil leaves
1 egg
1 teaspoon water
4 boneless skinless chicken breast halves
3 tablespoons olive oil, divided
¾ cup chopped onion
8 ounces cremini or button mushrooms, sliced
3 cloves garlic, minced
3 tablespoons all-purpose flour
1 can (14½ ounces) chicken broth
½ cup dry marsala wine
¾ teaspoon salt
¼ teaspoon ground black pepper
Chopped fresh parsley (optional)

Preheat oven to 375°F. Spray 11×7-inch baking dish with nonstick cooking spray.

Cook noodles according to package directions. Drain and place in prepared dish.

*continued on page 112*

*Chicken Marsala*

*Chicken Marsala, continued*

Meanwhile, combine bread crumbs and basil on shallow plate or pie plate. Beat egg with water on another shallow plate or pie plate. Dip chicken in egg mixture, letting excess drip off. Roll in crumb mixture, patting to coat.

Heat 2 tablespoons oil in large skillet over medium-high heat until hot. Cook chicken 3 minutes per side or until browned. Transfer to clean plate; set aside.

Heat remaining 1 tablespoon oil in same skillet over medium heat. Add onion; cook and stir 5 minutes. Add mushrooms and garlic; cook and stir 3 minutes. Sprinkle onion mixture with flour; cook and stir 1 minute. Add broth, wine, salt and pepper; bring to a boil over high heat. Cook and stir 5 minutes or until sauce thickens.

Reserve ½ cup sauce. Pour remaining sauce over noodles; stir until noodles are well coated. Place chicken on top of noodles. Spoon reserved sauce over chicken.

Bake, uncovered, about 20 minutes or until chicken is no longer pink in centers and sauce is hot and bubbly. Sprinkle with parsley, if desired.

*Makes 4 servings*

# TOMATO, BASIL & BROCCOLI CHICKEN

❤ ❤ ❤

4 **boneless skinless chicken breast halves**
   **Salt and black pepper (optional)**
2 **tablespoons margarine or butter**
1 **package (6.9 ounces) RICE-A-RONI® Chicken Flavor**
1 **teaspoon dried basil leaves**
2 **cups broccoli florets**
1 **medium tomato, seeded, chopped**
1 **cup (4 ounces) shredded mozzarella cheese**

1. Sprinkle chicken with salt and pepper, if desired.

2. In large skillet, melt margarine over medium-high heat. Add chicken; cook 2 minutes on each side or until browned. Remove from skillet; set aside, reserving drippings. Keep warm.

3. In same skillet, sauté rice-vermicelli mix in reserved drippings over medium heat until vermicelli is golden brown. Stir in 2½ cups water, contents of seasoning packet and basil. Place chicken over rice mixture; bring to a boil over high heat.

4. Cover; reduce heat. Simmer 15 minutes. Top with broccoli and tomato.

5. Cover; continue to simmer 5 minutes or until liquid is absorbed and chicken is no longer pink in center. Sprinkle with cheese. Cover; let stand a few minutes before serving.                    *Makes 4 servings*

# CHICKEN MILANO

♥ ♥ ♥

2 cloves garlic, minced
4 boneless skinless chicken breast halves
   (about 1¼ pounds)
½ teaspoon dried basil leaves, crushed
⅛ teaspoon crushed red pepper flakes (optional)
   Salt and black pepper
1 tablespoon olive oil
1 can (14½ ounces) DEL MONTE® Diced Tomatoes with
   Basil, Garlic & Oregano
1 can (14½ ounces) DEL MONTE® Cut Green Italian
   Beans, drained
¼ cup whipping cream

1. Rub garlic over chicken. Sprinkle with basil and red pepper. Season with salt and black pepper.

2. Brown chicken in oil in skillet over medium-high heat. Stir in tomatoes.

3. Cover; simmer 5 minutes. Uncover; reduce heat to medium and cook 8 to 10 minutes or until liquid is slightly thickened and chicken is tender.

4. Stir in green beans and cream; heat through. Do not boil.

*Makes 4 servings*

**Prep and Cook Time:** 25 minutes

*Chicken Milano*

# WALNUT CHICKEN

♥ ♥ ♥

1 pound boneless skinless chicken thighs
3 tablespoons soy sauce
2 tablespoons minced fresh ginger
1 tablespoon cornstarch
1 tablespoon rice wine
2 cloves garlic, minced
¼ to ½ teaspoon red pepper flakes
3 tablespoons vegetable oil
½ cup walnut halves or pieces
1 cup frozen cut green beans, thawed
½ cup sliced water chestnuts
2 green onions with tops, cut into 1-inch pieces
¼ cup water
Hot cooked rice

1. Rinse chicken and pat dry with paper towels. Cut into 1-inch cubes. Combine soy sauce, ginger, cornstarch, wine, garlic and red pepper in large bowl; stir until smooth. Add chicken; toss. Marinate 10 minutes.

2. Heat wok or large skillet over high heat about 1 minute or until hot. Drizzle oil into wok and heat 30 seconds. Add walnuts; stir-fry about 1 minute or until lightly browned. Remove to small bowl. Add chicken mixture to wok; stir-fry about 5 to 7 minutes or until chicken is no longer pink in center. Add beans, water chestnuts, onions and water; stir-fry until heated through. Serve over rice. Sprinkle with walnuts.

*Makes 4 servings*

*Walnut Chicken*

# HOMESTYLE CHICKEN POT PIE

♥ ♥ ♥

2 tablespoons butter or margarine, divided
1 pound boneless skinless chicken breasts, cut into
   1-inch pieces
½ teaspoon *each* salt and ground black pepper
1 package (16 ounces) frozen mixed vegetables, such as
   potatoes, peas and carrots, thawed and drained
1 can (10¾ ounces) condensed cream of chicken soup,
   undiluted
⅓ cup dry white wine or milk
1 refrigerated ready rolled pie crust, at room
   temperature

1. Preheat oven to 425°F. Melt 1 tablespoon butter in medium broilerproof skillet over medium-high heat. Add chicken; sprinkle with salt and pepper. Cook 1 minute, stirring frequently. Reduce heat to medium-low. Stir in vegetables, soup and wine; simmer 5 minutes.

2. While soup mixture is simmering, unwrap pie crust. Using small cookie cutter, make 4 decorative cut-outs from pastry to allow steam to escape. Remove chicken mixture from heat; top with pie crust. Melt remaining tablespoon butter. Brush pie crust with 2 teaspoons melted butter. Arrange cut-outs attractively over crust, if desired. Brush cut-outs with remaining 1 teaspoon melted butter. Bake 12 minutes. Turn oven to broil; broil 4 to 5 inches from heat source 2 minutes or until crust is golden brown and chicken mixture is bubbly.

*Makes 4 to 5 servings*

*Homestyle Chicken Pot Pie*

# CHICKEN IN FRENCH ONION SAUCE

♥ ♥ ♥

1 package (10 ounces) frozen baby carrots, thawed and
  drained *or* 4 medium carrots, cut into strips
  (about 2 cups)
2 cups sliced mushrooms
½ cup thinly sliced celery
1⅓ cups FRENCH'S® French Fried Onions, divided
4 chicken breast halves, skinned and boned
½ cup white wine
¾ cup prepared chicken bouillon
½ teaspoon garlic salt
½ teaspoon pepper
  Paprika

Preheat oven to 375°F. In 12×8-inch baking dish, combine vegetables and
⅔ *cup* French Fried Onions. Arrange chicken breasts on vegetables. In
small bowl, combine wine, bouillon, garlic salt and pepper; pour over
chicken and vegetables. Sprinkle chicken with paprika. Bake, covered, at
375°F for 35 minutes or until chicken is done. Baste chicken with wine
sauce and top with remaining ⅔ *cup* onions; bake, uncovered, 3 minutes or
until onions are golden brown.                              *Makes 4 servings*

*Chicken in French Onion Sauce*

# PAELLA

❤ ❤ ❤

- 1 tablespoon olive oil
- ½ pound chicken breast cubes
- 1 cup uncooked rice*
- 1 medium onion, chopped
- 1 clove garlic, minced
- 1½ cups chicken broth
- 1 can (8 ounces) stewed tomatoes, chopped, undrained
- ½ teaspoon paprika
- ⅛ to ¼ teaspoon ground red pepper
- ⅛ teaspoon ground saffron
- ½ pound medium shrimp, peeled and deveined
- 1 small red pepper, cut into strips
- 1 small green pepper, cut into strips
- ½ cup frozen green peas

*If using medium grain rice, use 1¼ cups of broth; if using parboiled rice, use 1¾ cups of broth.

Heat oil in Dutch oven over medium-high heat until hot. Add chicken and stir until browned. Add rice, onion, and garlic. Cook, stirring, until onion is tender and rice is lightly browned. Add broth, tomatoes, tomato liquid, paprika, ground red pepper, and saffron. Bring to a boil; stir. Reduce heat; cover and simmer 10 minutes. Add shrimp, pepper strips and peas. Cover and simmer 10 minutes or until rice is tender and liquid is absorbed.

*Makes 6 servings*

*Favorite recipe from* **USA Rice Federation**

*Paella*

# TURKEY-OLIVE RAGOÛT EN CRUST

♥ ♥ ♥

½ pound boneless white or dark turkey meat, cut into
    1-inch cubes
1 clove garlic, minced
1 teaspoon vegetable oil
¼ cup (about 10) small whole frozen onions
½ cup reduced-sodium chicken bouillon or turkey broth
½ teaspoon dried parsley flakes
⅛ teaspoon dried thyme leaves
1 small bay leaf
1 medium red potato, skin on, cut into ½-inch cubes
10 frozen snow peas
8 whole small pitted ripe olives
1 can (4 ounces) refrigerated crescent rolls
½ teaspoon dried dill weed

1. Preheat oven to 375°F.

2. In medium skillet over medium heat, cook and stir turkey in garlic and oil 3 to 4 minutes or until no longer pink; remove and set aside. Add onions to skillet; cook and stir until lightly browned. Add bouillon, parsley, thyme, bay leaf and potato. Bring mixture to a boil. Reduce heat; cover and simmer 10 minutes or until potato is tender. Remove and discard bay leaf.

3. Combine turkey mixture with potato mixture. Stir in snow peas and olives. Divide mixture between 2 (1¾-cup) individual ovenproof casseroles.

*continued on page 126*

*Turkey-Olive Ragoût en Crust*

4. Divide crescent rolls into 2 rectangles; press perforations together to seal. If necessary, roll out each rectangle to make dough large enough to cover top of each casserole. Sprinkle dough with dill weed, pressing lightly into dough. Cut small decorative shape from each dough piece; discard cutouts or place on baking sheet and bake in oven with casseroles. Place dough over turkey-vegetable mixture in casseroles. Trim dough to fit; press dough to edge of each casserole to seal. Bake 7 to 8 minutes or until pastry is golden brown. *Makes 2 individual deep-dish pies*

**Lattice Crust Variation:** With pastry wheel or knife, cut each rectangle lengthwise into 6 strips. Arrange strips, lattice-fashion, over turkey-vegetable mixture; trim dough to fit. Press ends of dough to edge of each casserole to seal.

**Note:** For more golden crust, brush top of dough with beaten egg yolk before baking.

*Favorite recipe from* **National Turkey Federation**

# TURKEY COTTAGE PIE

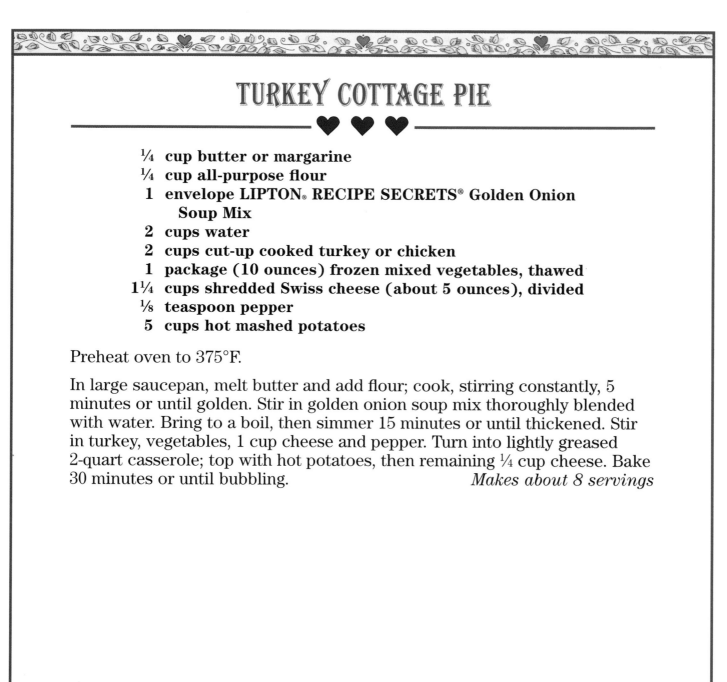

♥ ♥ ♥

¼ cup butter or margarine
¼ cup all-purpose flour
1 envelope LIPTON® RECIPE SECRETS® Golden Onion Soup Mix
2 cups water
2 cups cut-up cooked turkey or chicken
1 package (10 ounces) frozen mixed vegetables, thawed
1¼ cups shredded Swiss cheese (about 5 ounces), divided
⅛ teaspoon pepper
5 cups hot mashed potatoes

Preheat oven to 375°F.

In large saucepan, melt butter and add flour; cook, stirring constantly, 5 minutes or until golden. Stir in golden onion soup mix thoroughly blended with water. Bring to a boil, then simmer 15 minutes or until thickened. Stir in turkey, vegetables, 1 cup cheese and pepper. Turn into lightly greased 2-quart casserole; top with hot potatoes, then remaining ¼ cup cheese. Bake 30 minutes or until bubbling. *Makes about 8 servings*

# HEARTY NOODLE CASSEROLE

♥ ♥ ♥

1 jar (26½ ounces) spaghetti sauce
1 pound Italian sausage
1 pint (16 ounces) ricotta or cottage cheese
1 package (12 ounces) extra wide noodles, cooked
1 package (8 ounces) shredded mozzarella cheese,
  divided
1 can (4 ounces) sliced mushrooms
½ cup chopped green bell pepper

1. Preheat oven to 350°F. Cook sausage in large skillet over medium-high heat about 5 minutes or until no longer pink, stirring to separate.

2. Combine sauce, sausage, ricotta cheese, noodles, half the mozzarella cheese, mushrooms and bell pepper in large bowl. Spoon into 3-quart or 13×9-inch baking pan. Top with remaining mozzarella cheese.

3. Bake, uncovered, about 25 minutes or until heated through.

*Makes 4 to 6 servings*

*Hearty Noodle Casserole*

# CONTADINA® CLASSIC LASAGNE

❤ ❤ ❤

 1 pound dry lasagne noodles, cooked
 1 tablespoon olive or vegetable oil
 1 cup chopped onion
 ½ cup chopped green bell pepper
 2 cloves garlic, minced
 1½ pounds lean ground beef
 2 cans (14.5 ounces each) CONTADINA® Recipe Ready
    Diced Tomatoes, undrained
 1 can (8 ounces) CONTADINA® Tomato Sauce
 1 can (6 ounces) CONTADINA® Tomato Paste
 ½ cup dry red wine or beef broth
 1½ teaspoons salt
 1 teaspoon dried oregano leaves, crushed
 1 teaspoon dried basil leaves, crushed
 ½ teaspoon ground black pepper
 1 egg
 1 cup (8 ounces) ricotta cheese
 2 cups (8 ounces) shredded mozzarella cheese, divided

1. Cook pasta according to package directions; drain.

2. Meanwhile, heat oil in large skillet. Add onion, bell pepper and garlic; sauté for 3 minutes or until vegetables are tender.

3. Add beef; cook for 5 to 6 minutes or until evenly browned.

*continued on page 132*

*Contadina® Classic Lasagne*

*Contadina® Classic Lasagne, continued*

4. Add tomatoes and juice, tomato sauce, tomato paste, wine, salt, oregano, basil and black pepper; bring to a boil. Reduce heat to low; simmer, uncovered, for 20 minutes, stirring occasionally.

5. Beat egg slightly in medium bowl. Stir in ricotta cheese and 1 cup mozzarella cheese.

6. Layer noodles, half of meat sauce, noodles, all of ricotta cheese mixture, noodles and remaining meat sauce in ungreased 13×9-inch baking dish. Sprinkle with remaining mozzarella cheese.

7. Bake in preheated 350°F oven for 25 to 30 minutes or until heated through. Let stand for 10 minutes before cutting to serve.

*Makes 10 servings*

**Prep Time:** 35 minutes
**Cook Time:** 30 minutes
**Standing Time:** 10 minutes

*Grandma's Secret: Homemade garlic bread and a tossed salad of garden vegetables nicely complement this tried and true family favorite.*

# OVEN-EASY BEEF & POTATO DINNER

♥ ♥ ♥

    4  cups frozen hash brown potatoes, thawed
    3  tablespoons vegetable oil
    ⅛  teaspoon pepper
    1  pound ground beef
    1  cup water
    1  package (about ¾ ounce) brown gravy mix
    ½  teaspoon garlic salt
    1  package (10 ounces) frozen mixed vegetables, thawed
        and drained
    1  cup (4 ounces) shredded Cheddar cheese, divided
  1⅓  cup FRENCH'S® French Fried Onions, divided

Preheat oven to 400°F. In 12×8-inch baking dish, combine potatoes, oil and pepper. Firmly press potato mixture evenly across bottom and up sides of dish to form a shell. Bake, uncovered, at 400°F for 15 minutes. Meanwhile, in large skillet, brown ground beef; drain. Stir in water, gravy mix and garlic salt; bring to a boil. Add mixed vegetables; reduce heat to medium and cook, uncovered, 5 minutes. Remove from heat and stir in ½ cup cheese and ⅔ cup French Fried Onions; spoon into hot potato shell. *Reduce oven temperature to 350°F.* Bake, uncovered, at 350°F for 15 minutes or until heated through. Top with remaining cheese and ⅔ cup onions; bake, uncovered, 5 minutes or until onions are golden brown.

*Makes 4 to 6 servings*

# OLD-FASHIONED BEEF POT PIE

♥ ♥ ♥

- 1 pound ground beef
- 1 can (11 ounces) condensed beef with vegetables and barley soup
- ½ cup water
- 1 package (10 ounces) frozen peas and carrots, thawed and drained
- ½ teaspoon seasoned salt
- ⅛ teaspoon garlic powder
- ⅛ teaspoon ground black pepper
- 1 cup (4 ounces) shredded Cheddar cheese, divided
- 1⅓ cups FRENCH'S® French Fried Onions, divided
- 1 package (7.5 ounces) refrigerated biscuits

Preheat oven to 350°F. In large skillet, brown ground beef in large chunks; drain. Stir in soup, water, vegetables and seasonings; bring to a boil. Reduce heat and simmer, uncovered, 5 minutes. Remove from heat; stir in ½ cup cheese and *⅔ cup* French Fried Onions.

Pour mixture into 12×8-inch baking dish. Cut each biscuit in half; place, cut side down, around edge of casserole. Bake, uncovered, 15 to 20 minutes or until biscuits are done. Top with remaining cheese and *⅔ cup* onions; bake, uncovered, 5 minutes or until onions are golden brown.

*Makes 4 to 6 servings*

*Old-Fashioned Beef Pot Pie*

# BEEFY NACHO CRESCENT BAKE

### ♥ ♥ ♥

1 pound lean ground beef
½ cup chopped onion
¼ teaspoon salt
⅛ teaspoon ground black pepper
1 tablespoon chili powder
1 teaspoon ground cumin
1 teaspoon dried oregano leaves
1 can (11 ounces) condensed nacho cheese soup,
   undiluted
1 cup milk
1 can (8 ounces) refrigerated crescent roll dough
¼ cup (1 ounce) shredded Cheddar cheese
   Chopped fresh cilantro (optional)
   Salsa (optional)

Preheat oven to 375°F. Spray 13×9-inch baking dish with nonstick cooking spray.

Place beef and onion in large skillet; season with salt and pepper. Brown beef over medium-high heat until no longer pink, stirring to separate meat. Drain fat. Stir in chili powder, cumin and oregano. Cook and stir 2 minutes; remove from heat.

Combine soup and milk in medium bowl, stirring until smooth. Pour soup mixture into prepared dish, spreading evenly.

*continued on page 138*

*Beefy Nacho Crescent Bake*

*Beefy Nacho Crescent Bake, continued*

Separate crescent dough into 4 rectangles; press perforations together firmly. Roll each rectangle to 8×4 inches. Cut each rectangle in half crosswise to form 8 (4-inch) squares.

Spoon about ¼ cup beef mixture in center of each square. Lift 4 corners of dough up over filling to meet in center; pinch and twist firmly to seal. Place squares in dish.

Bake, uncovered, 20 to 25 minutes or until crusts are golden brown. Sprinkle cheese over squares. Bake 5 minutes or until cheese melts. To serve, spoon soup mixture in dish over each serving; sprinkle with cilantro, if desired. Serve with salsa, if desired. *Makes 4 servings*

*Grandma's Secret: For a spicier version of this southwestern favorite, substitute Monteray Jack cheese with jalapeño peppers for the Cheddar cheese and serve with a hot and spicy salsa, if desired.*

# PATCHWORK CASSEROLE

♥ ♥ ♥

    2  pounds ground beef
    2  cups chopped green bell pepper
    1  cup chopped onion
    2  pounds frozen Southern-style hash-brown potatoes,
         thawed
    2  cans (8 ounces each) tomato sauce
    1  cup water
    1  can (6 ounces) tomato paste
    1  teaspoon salt
    ½  teaspoon dried basil, crumbled
    ¼  teaspoon ground black pepper
    1  pound pasteurized process American cheese, thinly
         sliced

Preheat oven to 350°F.

Brown beef in large skillet over medium heat about 10 minutes; drain off fat.

Add bell pepper and onion; cook and stir until tender, about 4 minutes. Stir in potatoes, tomato sauce, water, tomato paste, salt, basil and black pepper.

Spoon half of mixture into 13×9×2-inch baking pan or 3-quart baking dish; top with half of cheese. Spoon remaining meat mixture evenly on top of cheese. Cover pan with aluminum foil. Bake 45 minutes.

Cut remaining cheese into decorative shapes; place on top of casserole. Let stand loosely covered until cheese melts, about 5 minutes.

*Makes 8 to 10 servings*

# SALISBURY STEAKS WITH MUSHROOM-WINE SAUCE

♥ ♥ ♥

1   **pound lean ground beef sirloin**
¾   **teaspoon garlic salt or seasoned salt**
¼   **teaspoon ground black pepper**
2   **tablespoons butter or margarine**
1   **package (8 ounces) sliced button mushrooms** *or*
    **2 packages (4 ounces each) sliced exotic mushrooms**
2   **tablespoons sweet vermouth or ruby port wine**
1   **jar (12 ounces)** *or* **1 can (10½ ounces) beef gravy**

1. Heat large heavy nonstick skillet over medium-high heat 3 minutes or until hot.* Meanwhile, combine ground sirloin, garlic salt and pepper; mix well. Shape mixture into four ¼-inch-thick oval patties.

2. Place Patties in skillet as they are formed; cook 3 minutes per side or until browned. Transfer to plate. Pour off drippings.

3. Melt butter in skillet; add mushrooms. Cook and stir 2 minutes. Add vermouth; cook 1 minute. Add gravy; mix well.

4. Return patties to skillet; simmer uncovered over medium heat 2 minutes for medium or until desired doneness, turning meat and stirring sauce.

*Makes 4 servings*

*If pan is not heavy, use medium heat.

*Salisbury Steaks with Mushroom-Wine Sauce*

# STRING PIE

❤ ❤ ❤

1 pound ground beef
½ cup chopped onion
¼ cup chopped green pepper
1 jar (15½ ounces) spaghetti sauce
8 ounces spaghetti, cooked and drained
⅓ cup grated Parmesan cheese
2 eggs, beaten
2 teaspoons butter
1 cup cottage cheese
½ cup (2 ounces) shredded mozzarella cheese

Preheat oven to 350°F. Cook beef, onion and green pepper in large skillet over medium-high heat until meat is browned. Drain fat. Stir in spaghetti sauce. Combine spaghetti, Parmesan cheese, eggs and butter in large bowl; mix well. Place in bottom of 13×9-inch baking pan. Spread cottage cheese over top; cover with sauce mixture. Sprinkle with mozzarella cheese. Bake until mixture is thoroughly heated and cheese is melted, about 20 minutes.

*Makes 6 to 8 servings*

*Favorite recipe from* **North Dakota Beef Commission**

*String Pie*

# LAMB & STUFFING DINNER CASSEROLE

♥ ♥ ♥

2 tablespoons margarine
1 cup chopped onion
1 clove garlic, minced
1 can (14 ounces) reduced-sodium chicken broth, divided
1 cup coarsely shredded carrots
¼ cup fresh parsley, minced *or* 1 tablespoon dried parsley
   flakes
12 ounces cooked fresh American lamb, cut into cubes *or*
   1 pound ground American lamb, cooked and drained
1 (6-ounce) box herb-flavored stuffing mix
1 (8-ounce) can whole tomatoes, drained and chopped

Melt margarine over medium heat; sauté onion and garlic 1 minute. Add ¼ cup of broth, carrots and parsley. Cover and cook until carrots are crisp-tender, about 5 minutes. In large bowl, lightly combine lamb and stuffing mix. Add vegetable mixture, remaining broth and tomatoes. Toss lightly until well mixed.

Spoon lamb mixture into greased 8×8×2-inch baking dish. Cover and bake at 375°F for 20 minutes or until heated through.          *Makes 6 servings*

*Favorite recipe from **American Lamb Council***

# EASY LAMB AND POTATO BAKE

♥ ♥ ♥

Nonstick cooking spray
4 lamb shoulder blade chops or leg steaks, ¾-inch thick
   (1½ pounds), trimmed
2 tablespoons cornmeal
4 teaspoons water
1 tablespoon prepared mustard
1 package (about 5 ounces) scalloped potato mix
1 teaspoon caraway seeds

Spray large skillet with nonstick spray. Brown lamb over medium-high heat about 5 minutes on each side. In small bowl, combine cornmeal, water and mustard; mix well. In 8×8×2-inch inch baking dish, prepare scalloped potato mix according to package directions, except omit margarine and add caraway seeds. Spread mustard mixture on surface of browned chops; place mustard-side up on top of dried potato mixture. Bake, uncovered, in 400°F oven about 35 minutes or until lightly browned. Remove from oven; let stand 5 minutes. Serve with steamed green vegetable or crisp green salad.

*Makes 4 servings*

**Prep Time:** 20 minutes
**Cook Time:** 35 minutes

*Favorite recipe from* **American Lamb Council**

# FETTUCCINE WITH GORGONZOLA SAUCE

♥ ♥ ♥

        8  ounces fettuccine
        2  teaspoons olive oil
       ½  pound asparagus, cut into 1-inch pieces
        1  leek, cut into ½-inch pieces
        1  medium red bell pepper, cut into short strips
        2  cloves garlic, minced
        1  can (15 ounces) artichoke hearts, drained and
              quartered
        1  cup cherry tomato halves
           Gorgonzola Sauce (page 148)
       ¼  cup grated Parmesan cheese or crumbled Gorgonzola
           Cherry tomatoes for garnish

1. Cook fettuccine according to package directions. Drain in colander. Place in large warm bowl; keep warm.

2. Meanwhile, heat oil in large skillet over medium heat. Add asparagus, leek, pepper and garlic; cook and stir 5 to 7 minutes or until asparagus is crisp-tender. Add artichoke hearts and tomatoes; cook 2 to 3 minutes or until hot. Add to fettuccine.

3. Prepare Gorgonzola Sauce.

4. Pour Gorgonzola Sauce over fettuccine; toss. Sprinkle with Parmesan cheese. Garnish, if desired.                    *Makes 4 servings*

*continued on page 148*

*Fettuccine with Gorgonzola Sauce*

*Fettuccine with Gorgonzola Sauce, continued*

## GORGONZOLA SAUCE

- **3  tablespoons butter or margarine**
- **¼  cup all-purpose flour**
- **2  cups milk**
- **¼  cup vegetable broth**
- **½  teaspoon ground black pepper**
- **4  ounces Gorgonzola, crumbled**

1. Melt butter in small saucepan over medium heat. Stir in flour. Cook and stir 2 to 3 minutes or until bubbly. Gradually stir in milk, broth and pepper. Cook until thickened, stirring constantly.

2. Reduce heat to low. Stir in cheese until melted.     *Makes about 2½ cups*

*Grandma's Secret:* Gorgonzola is a rich and creamy Italian cheese that takes its name from the town where it was originally made. The longer the cheese ages, the stronger its aroma becomes.

# CHEESE POLENTA

♥ ♥ ♥

    1  cup cold water
    1  cup yellow cornmeal
 1½  cups boiling water
    2  to 4 tablespoons crumbled Gorgonzola
    1  clove garlic, minced
    1  teaspoon salt

Stir water into cornmeal in large saucepan. Heat over medium heat until warm. Slowly stir in boiling water. Bring to a boil over medium-high heat. Reduce heat to low. Cook 15 minutes or until mixture is thick, stirring constantly. Stir in cheese, garlic and salt. Pour into greased 8-inch round pan; let stand 10 minutes or until firm.

*Grandma's Secret: Polenta is easy to make and complements many savory dishes. Serve it with a vegetable medley for a fast and healthful vegetarian dinner.*

# BROCCOLI LASAGNA

♥ ♥ ♥

1 tablespoon CRISCO® Oil* plus additional for oiling
1 cup chopped onion
3 cloves garlic, minced
1 can (14½ ounces) no salt added tomatoes, undrained
   and chopped
1 can (8 ounces) no salt added tomato sauce
1 can (6 ounces) no salt added tomato paste
1 cup thinly sliced fresh mushrooms
¼ cup chopped fresh parsley
1 tablespoon red wine vinegar
1 teaspoon dried oregano leaves
1 teaspoon dried basil leaves
1 bay leaf
½ teaspoon salt
¼ teaspoon crushed red pepper
1½ cups lowfat cottage cheese
1 cup (4 ounces) shredded low moisture part-skim
   mozzarella cheese, divided
6 lasagna noodles, cooked (without salt or fat) and well
   drained
3 cups chopped broccoli, cooked and well drained
1 tablespoon grated Parmesan cheese

*Any other Crisco® Oil can be substituted.

*continued on page 152*

*Broccoli Lasagna*

*Broccoli Lasagna, continued*

1. Heat oven to 350°F. Oil 11¾×7½×2-inch baking dish lightly.

2. Heat 1 tablespoon Crisco® Oil in large saucepan on medium heat. Add onion and garlic. Cook and stir until tender. Stir in tomatoes, tomato sauce, tomato paste, mushrooms, parsley, vinegar, oregano, basil, bay leaf, salt and crushed red pepper. Bring to a boil. Reduce heat to low. Cover. Simmer 30 minutes, stirring occasionally. Remove bay leaf.

3. Combine cottage cheese and ½ cup mozzarella cheese in small bowl. Stir well.

4. Place 2 lasagna noodles in bottom of baking dish. Layer with one cup broccoli, one-third of the tomato sauce and one-third of the cottage cheese mixture. Repeat layers. Cover with foil.

5. Bake at 350°F for 25 minutes. Uncover. Sprinkle with remaining ½ cup mozzarella cheese and Parmesan cheese. Bake, uncovered, 10 minutes or until cheese melts. *Do not overbake.* Let stand 10 minutes before serving.

*Makes 8 servings*

# BROCCOLI & CHEDDAR NOODLE CASSEROLE

♥ ♥ ♥

1 package (12 ounces) dry wide egg noodles
3 tablespoons margarine or butter, divided
2 cups chopped onions
4 cups broccoli flowerets
1 can (14.5 ounces) CONTADINA® Stewed Tomatoes, undrained
1 can (6 ounces) CONTADINA® Tomato Paste
1 package (1½ ounces) spaghetti sauce seasoning mix
2 cups water
1 teaspoon garlic salt
1½ cups (6 ounces) shredded Cheddar cheese
½ cup CONTADINA® Seasoned Bread Crumbs

1. Cook noodles according to package directions; drain.

2. Meanwhile, melt 2 tablespoons margarine in 5-quart saucepan; sauté onions until tender.

3. Stir in broccoli, tomatoes and juice, tomato paste, seasoning mix, water, and garlic salt. Bring to a boil. Reduce heat; simmer, uncovered, for 10 minutes, stirring occasionally. Stir in cooked noodles.

4. Layer half of the noodle mixture in 13×9×2-inch baking dish. Sprinkle with cheese. Layer with remaining noodle mixture.

5. Melt remaining 1 tablespoon margarine; stir in crumbs. Sprinkle over casserole; cover and bake in preheated 350°F oven 20 minutes. Uncover; bake 5 minutes.

*Makes 6 servings*

# CLASSIC FETTUCCINE ALFREDO

❤ ❤ ❤

¾ pound uncooked fettuccine
6 tablespoons unsalted butter
⅔ cup heavy or whipping cream
½ teaspoon salt
  Dash *each* white pepper and ground nutmeg
1 cup (about 3 ounces) freshly grated Parmesan cheese
2 tablespoons chopped fresh parsley
  Fresh Italian parsley sprig for garnish (optional)

1. Cook fettuccine according to package directions; drain. Set aside in large saucepan.

2. Place butter and cream in large, heavy skillet over medium-low heat. Cook and stir until butter melts and mixture bubbles. Cook and stir 2 minutes more. Stir in salt, pepper and nutmeg. Remove from heat. Gradually stir in cheese until thoroughly blended and smooth. Return briefly to heat to blend cheese completely if necessary. (Do not let sauce bubble or cheese will become lumpy and tough.)

3. Pour sauce over fettuccine in pan. Stir and toss with 2 forks over low heat 2 to 3 minutes until sauce is thickened and fettuccine is evenly coated. Sprinkle with chopped parsley. Garnish, if desired. Serve immediately.

*Makes 4 servings*

*Classic Fettuccine Alfredo*

# Potato Passion

## ONION-ROASTED POTATOES
♥ ♥ ♥

1 envelope LIPTON® RECIPE SECRETS® Onion Soup Mix
4 medium all-purpose potatoes, cut into large chunks
   (about 2 pounds)
⅓ cup olive or vegetable oil

1. Preheat oven to 450°F. In large plastic bag or bowl, add all ingredients. Close bag and shake, or toss in bowl, until potatoes are evenly coated.

2. In 13×9-inch baking or roasting pan, arrange potatoes; discard bag.

3. Bake uncovered, stirring occasionally, 40 minutes or until potatoes are tender and golden brown. *Makes 4 servings*

**Tip:** *Also terrific with LIPTON® RECIPE SECRETS® Garlic Mushroom, Onion-Mushroom, Golden Onion or Savory Herb with Garlic.

*Onion-Roasted Potatoes*

# SWEET POTATO GRATIN

♥ ♥ ♥

3 pounds sweet potatoes (about 5 large), unpeeled
½ cup butter or margarine, divided
¼ cup plus 2 tablespoons packed light brown sugar, divided
2 eggs
⅔ cup orange juice
2 teaspoons ground cinnamon, divided
½ teaspoon salt
¼ teaspoon ground nutmeg
⅓ cup all-purpose flour
¼ cup uncooked old-fashioned oats
⅓ cup chopped pecans or walnuts

Preheat oven to 350°F. Bake sweet potatoes about 1 hour or until tender. Or, pierce sweet potatoes several times with table fork and place on microwavable plate. Microwave at HIGH 16 to 18 minutes, rotating and turning over potatoes after 9 minutes. Let stand 5 minutes.

Cut hot sweet potatoes lengthwise into halves. Scrape hot pulp from skins into large bowl.

Beat ¼ cup butter and 2 tablespoons sugar into sweet potatoes with electric mixer at medium speed until butter is melted. Add eggs, orange juice, 1½ teaspoons cinnamon, salt and nutmeg. Beat until smooth. Pour mixture into 1½-quart baking dish or gratin dish; smooth top.

*continued on page 160*

*Sweet Potato Gratin*

*Sweet Potato Gratin, continued*

For topping, combine flour, oats, remaining ¼ cup sugar and remaining ½ teaspoon cinnamon in medium bowl. Cut in remaining ¼ cup butter until mixture resembles coarse crumbs. Stir in pecans. Sprinkle topping evenly over sweet potatoes.*

Bake 25 to 30 minutes or until sweet potatoes are heated through. For crisper topping, broil 5 inches from heat 2 to 3 minutes or until golden brown.

*Makes 6 to 8 servings*

*At this point, Sweet Potato Gratin may be covered and refrigerated up to 1 day. Let stand at room temperature 1 hour before baking.

*Grandma's Secret: Sweet potatoes are native to North America and have become a traditional Thanksgiving Day favorite. This root vegetable is not truly a potato, but a member of the morning glory family. Like carrots, sweet potatoes are an excellent source of beta-carotene.*

# DOUBLE CHEDDAR BACON MASHED POTATOES

♥ ♥ ♥

    2    pounds all-purpose potatoes, peeled and sliced
    1    jar (16 ounces) Ragú® Cheese Creations!® Double
         Cheddar Sauce, heated
    5    slices bacon, crisp-cooked and crumbled (about ¼ cup)
    1    teaspoon salt

1. In 3-quart saucepan, cover potatoes with water. Bring to a boil over high heat. Reduce heat to low and simmer uncovered 15 minutes or until potatoes are very tender; drain. Return potatoes to saucepan. Mash potatoes.

2. Stir Ragú Cheese Creations! Sauce into mashed potatoes. Stir in bacon and salt.

*Makes 6 servings*

**Tip:** Stir in ¼ cup chopped green onions for an extra flavor boost.

**Prep Time:** 10 minutes
**Cook Time:** 20 minutes

# POTATO SKINS WITH CHEDDAR MELT

### ❤ ❤ ❤

4   medium-size Idaho baking potatoes (about 2 pounds)
4   slices lean turkey bacon
2   tablespoons vegetable oil
2   cups (8 ounces) shredded ALPINE LACE® Reduced Fat
      Cheddar Cheese
¼   cup fat free sour cream
2   tablespoons finely chopped chives or green onions
1   tablespoon minced jalapeño pepper

1. Place a piece of foil on the bottom rack of the oven and preheat the oven to 425°F. Scrub the potatoes well and pierce the skins a few times with a sharp knife. Place the potatoes directly on the middle oven rack and bake for 1 hour or until soft.

2. Meanwhile, in a small skillet, cook the bacon over medium heat until crisp. Drain on paper towels, then crumble the bacon.

3. Using a sharp knife, cut the potatoes in half lengthwise. With a small spoon, scoop out the pulp, leaving a ¼-inch-thick shells. (Save the potato pulp for another use.) Cut the skins into appetizer-size triangles.

4. Place the skins on a baking sheet, brush the insides with the oil and bake for 15 minutes or until crisp.

5. Remove the skins from the oven, sprinkle with the cheese and return to the oven for 5 minutes or until the cheese melts. Top the skins with the sour cream, then sprinkle with the chives, pepper and bacon.

*Makes about 24 servings*

*Potato Skins with Cheddar Melt*

# POTATO GORGONZOLA GRATIN

♥ ♥ ♥

1   pound (2 medium-large) Colorado baking potatoes,
     unpeeled and very thinly sliced, divided
    Salt
    Ground black pepper
    Ground nutmeg
½   medium onion, thinly sliced
1   medium tart green apple, such as pippin or Granny
     Smith, *or* 1 medium pear, unpeeled, cored and very
     thinly sliced
1   cup low-fat milk or half-and-half
¾   cup (3 ounces) Gorgonzola or other blue cheese,
     crumbled
2   tablespoons freshly grated Parmesan cheese

Preheat oven to 400°F. In 8- or 9-inch square baking dish, arrange half the potatoes. Season generously with salt and pepper; sprinkle lightly with nutmeg. Top with onion and apple. Arrange remaining potatoes on top. Season again with salt and pepper; add milk. Cover dish with aluminum foil. Bake 30 to 40 minutes or until potatoes are tender. Remove foil; top with both cheeses. Bake, uncovered, 10 to 15 minutes or until top is lightly browned.                    *Makes 4 to 6 servings*

*Favorite recipe from* **Colorado Potato Administrative Committee**

*Potato Gorgonzola Gratin*

# GRILLED SWEET POTATO PACKETS WITH PECAN BUTTER

♥ ♥ ♥

4  sweet potatoes (about 8 ounces each), peeled and cut
    into ¼-inch-thick slices
1  large sweet or Spanish onion, thinly sliced and
    separated into rings
3  tablespoons vegetable oil
⅓  cup butter or margarine, softened
2  tablespoons packed light brown sugar
¼  teaspoon salt
¼  teaspoon ground cinnamon
¼  cup chopped pecans, toasted

1. Prepare barbecue grill for direct cooking.

2. Alternately place potato slices and onion rings on four 14×12-inch sheets of heavy-duty foil. Brush tops and sides with oil to prevent drying.

3. Wrap in foil. Place foil packets on grid. Grill packets, on covered grill, over medium coals 25 to 30 minutes or until potatoes are fork-tender.

4. Meanwhile, to prepare Pecan Butter, combine butter, sugar, salt and cinnamon in small bowl; mix well. Stir in pecans. Open packets carefully; top each with dollop of Pecan Butter.                    *Makes 4 servings*

*Grilled Sweet Potato Packets*
*with Pecan Butter*

# SONORA-STYLE BAKED POTATOES

♥ ♥ ♥

4 large baking potatoes, scrubbed
1 tablespoon vegetable oil
1 medium onion, chopped
2 cloves garlic, finely chopped
1 red or green bell pepper, seeded and chopped
1 can (15½ ounces) chili beans in mild or hot chili sauce, undrained
1 package (12 ounces) HEBREW NATIONAL® Jalapeño Beef Knockwurst, cut into ½-inch pieces
¼ cup chopped fresh cilantro

Prick potatoes in several places with tines of fork. Place on paper towel. Microwave on HIGH 8 minutes. Rearrange potatoes; cook 8 to 10 minutes or until potatoes are fork-tender.

Heat oil in large nonstick skillet over medium-high heat. Add onion and garlic; cook and stir 5 minutes. Add bell pepper; cook 2 minutes. Add beans and sausages; mix well. Reduce heat. Cover; simmer 10 minutes. Uncover; cook 1 to 2 minutes or until sauce thickens. Cut potatoes in half; top with sausage mixture. Sprinkle with cilantro. *Makes 4 servings*

# RUSTIC POTATOES AU GRATIN

♥ ♥ ♥

- ½ cup milk
- 1 can (10¾ ounces) condensed Cheddar cheese soup, undiluted
- 1 package (8 ounces) cream cheese, softened
- 1 clove garlic, minced
- ¼ teaspoon ground nutmeg
- ⅛ teaspoon ground black pepper
- 2 pounds baking potatoes, cut into ¼-inch slices
- 1 small onion, thinly sliced
- Paprika (optional)

**SLOW COOKER DIRECTIONS**

Heat milk in small saucepan over medium heat until small bubbles form around edge of pan. Remove from heat. Add soup, cheese, garlic, nutmeg and pepper. Stir until smooth. Layer ¼ of potatoes and ¼ of onion in bottom of slow cooker. Top with ¼ of soup mixture. Repeat layers 3 times, using remaining potatoes, onion and soup mixture. Cover and cook on LOW 6½ to 7 hours or until potatoes are tender and most of liquid is absorbed. Sprinkle with paprika, if desired. *Makes 6 servings*

# GARLIC MASHED POTATOES

♥ ♥ ♥

6 medium all-purpose potatoes, peeled, if desired, and
   cut into chunks (about 3 pounds)
  Water
1 envelope LIPTON® RECIPE SECRETS® Garlic
   Mushroom Soup Mix
½ cup milk
½ cup margarine or butter, softened

1. In 4-quart saucepan, cover potatoes with water; bring to a boil.

2. Reduce heat to low and simmer uncovered 20 minutes or until potatoes
are very tender; drain.

3. Return potatoes to saucepan, then mash. Stir in remaining ingredients.

*Makes 8 servings*

**Tip:** *Also terrific with LIPTON® RECIPE SECRETS® Savory Herb with
Garlic, Onion or Golden Onion Soup Mix.

*Garlic Mashed Potatoes*

# POTATO LATKES

❤ ❤ ❤

2  large or 3 medium baking potatoes (about 1¾ pounds),
   peeled and shredded
1  large onion (8 ounces), shredded
2  eggs, beaten
¼  cup matzo meal
¾  teaspoon salt
¼  teaspoon ground black pepper
2  tablespoons vegetable oil, divided
   Applesauce (optional)
   Sour cream (optional)

Combine potatoes and onion in large bowl. Add eggs, matzo meal, salt and pepper; mix well.

Heat 1 tablespoon oil in large skillet over medium-low heat until hot. Drop potato mixture by level ¼ cupfuls into skillet. Use back of spatula to flatten potato mixture into 3½-inch patties, about ½-inch thick. Cook about 4 minutes per side or until golden brown. Transfer to ovenproof platter lined with paper towels.

Keep warm in 200°F oven while preparing remaining latkes. Add remaining 1 tablespoon oil as needed. Serve warm with applesauce or sour cream. Garnish as desired.                                    *Makes about 18 latkes*

*Potato Latkes*

# POTATO AND PORK FRITTATA

### ♥ ♥ ♥

12 ounces (about 3 cups) frozen hash brown potatoes
1 teaspoon Cajun seasoning
4 egg whites
2 whole eggs
¼ cup low-fat (1%) milk
1 teaspoon dry mustard
¼ teaspoon ground black pepper
10 ounces (about 3 cups) frozen stir-fry vegetables
⅓ cup water
¾ cup chopped cooked lean pork
½ cup (2 ounces) shredded Cheddar cheese

1. Preheat oven to 400°F. Spray baking sheet with nonstick cooking spray. Spread potatoes on baking sheet; sprinkle with Cajun seasoning. Bake 15 minutes or until hot. Remove from oven. *Reduce oven temperature to 350°F.*

2. Beat egg whites, eggs, milk, mustard and pepper in small bowl. Place vegetables and water in medium ovenproof nonstick skillet. Cook over medium heat 5 minutes or until vegetables are crisp-tender; drain.

3. Add pork and potatoes to vegetables in skillet; stir lightly. Add egg mixture. Sprinkle with cheese. Cook over medium-low heat 5 minutes. Place skillet in 350°F oven and bake 5 minutes or until egg mixture is set and cheese is melted.

*Makes 4 servings*

*Potato and Pork Frittata*

# SKEWERED GRILLED POTATOES

♥ ♥ ♥

2   pounds red potatoes, quartered
⅓   cup cold water
½   cup MIRACLE WHIP® Salad Dressing
¼   cup dry white wine or chicken broth
2   teaspoons dried rosemary leaves, crushed
1   teaspoon garlic powder

• Place potatoes and water in 2-quart microwave-safe casserole; cover.

• Microwave on HIGH 12 to 15 minutes or until tender, stirring after 8 minutes. Drain.

• Mix remaining ingredients until well blended. Stir in potatoes. Refrigerate 1 hour. Drain, reserving marinade.

• Arrange potatoes on skewers. Place on grill over hot coals (coals will be glowing). Grill, covered, 6 to 8 minutes or until potatoes are tender and golden brown, brushing occasionally with reserved marinade and turning after 4 minutes.                                          *Makes 8 servings*

**Prep Time:** 20 minutes plus refrigerating
**Grill Time:** 8 minutes
**Microwave Time:** 15 minutes

# ROASTED GARLIC MASHED POTATOES

❤ ❤ ❤

1   large bulb garlic
    Olive oil
¼   cup chopped green onions
¼   cup margarine or butter
2½  pounds potatoes, peeled, cubed and cooked
1½  cups milk
½   cup GREY POUPON® Dijon Mustard
½   cup shredded Cheddar cheese (2 ounces)
¼   cup chopped parsley
    Salt and black pepper to taste

To roast garlic, peel off loose paperlike skin from bulb. Coat garlic bulb lightly with olive oil; wrap in foil. Place in small baking pan. Bake at 400°F for 40 to 45 minutes; cool. Separate cloves. Squeeze cloves to extract pulp; discard skins.

In large saucepan, over medium heat, sauté garlic pulp and green onions in margarine until tender. Add cooked potatoes, milk, mustard and cheese. Mash potato mixture until smooth and well blended. Stir in parsley; season with salt and pepper. Serve immediately.                    *Makes 8 servings*

# HERBED POTATO CHIPS

♥ ♥ ♥

Nonstick olive oil-flavored cooking spray
2 medium-sized red potatoes (about ½ pound), unpeeled
1 tablespoon olive oil
2 tablespoons minced fresh dill, thyme or rosemary *or*
  2 teaspoons dried dill weed, thyme or rosemary
¼ teaspoon garlic salt
⅛ teaspoon ground black pepper
1¼ cups nonfat sour cream

1. Preheat oven to 450°F. Spray large nonstick baking sheets with cooking spray; set aside.

2. Cut potatoes crosswise into very thin slices, about ⅟₁₆-inch thick. Pat dry with paper towels. Arrange potato slices in single layer on prepared baking sheets; coat potatoes with cooking spray.

3. Bake 10 minutes; turn slices over. Brush with oil. Combine dill, garlic salt and pepper in small bowl; sprinkle evenly onto potato slices. Continue baking 5 to 10 minutes or until potatoes are golden brown. Cool on baking sheets.

4. Serve with sour cream. *Makes about 60 chips*

*Herbed Potato Chips*

# OVEN ROASTED POTATOES AND ONIONS WITH HERBS

♥ ♥ ♥

3   pounds unpeeled red potatoes, cut into 1½-inch cubes
1   large sweet onion, such as Vadalia or Walla Walla, coarsely chopped
3   tablespoons olive oil
2   tablespoons butter, melted, or bacon drippings
3   cloves garlic, minced
¾   teaspoon salt
¾   teaspoon ground black pepper
⅓   cup packed chopped mixed fresh herbs, such as basil, chives, parsley, oregano, rosemary, sage, tarragon and thyme

1. Preheat oven to 450°F. Arrange potatoes and onion in large shallow roasting pan.

2. Combine oil, butter, garlic, salt and pepper in small bowl. Drizzle over potatoes and onion; toss well to combine.

3. Bake 30 minutes. Stir and bake 10 minutes more. Add herbs; toss well. Continue baking 10 to 15 minutes or until vegetables are tender and browned. Transfer to serving bowl. Garnish with fresh rosemary, if desired.

*Makes 6 servings*

*Oven Roasted Potatoes and Onions with Herbs*

# SWEET 'N' SASSY POTATO CASSEROLE

### ♥ ♥ ♥

  3  pounds sweet potatoes, peeled and cut into 1-inch
      pieces
  3  Anjou pears or tart apples, peeled and cut into 1-inch
      pieces
 ½  cup packed light brown sugar
 ½  cup maple or pancake syrup
  2  tablespoons FRANK'S® REDHOT® Hot Sauce
  2  teaspoons ground cinnamon
 ¼  teaspoon ground allspice
  2  tablespoons unsalted butter

1. Place sweet potatoes in large saucepan; cover with water. Bring to a boil. Cook 10 to 15 minutes or until tender. Drain. Place potatoes and pears in greased 3-quart baking dish.

2. Preheat oven to 400°F. Combine sugar, maple syrup, Redhot® sauce and spices in medium bowl. Pour over potatoes and pears. Dot with butter. Cover tightly.

3. Bake 30 to 35 minutes or until heated through and pears are tender. Baste mixture with sauce occasionally. Sprinkle with chopped toasted almonds, if desired.
*Makes 8 servings*

**Prep Time:** 25 minutes
**Cook Time:** 35 minutes

# CHEESE AND PEPPER STUFFED POTATO SKINS

♥ ♥ ♥

6 large russet potatoes (about ¾ pound each), scrubbed
4 tablespoons FRANK'S® REDHOT® Hot Sauce, divided
2 tablespoons butter, melted
1 large red bell pepper, seeded and finely chopped
1 cup chopped green onions
1 cup (4 ounces) shredded Cheddar cheese

1. Preheat oven to 450°F. Wrap potatoes in foil; bake about 1 hour 15 minutes or until fork tender. Let stand until cool enough to handle. Cut each potato in half lengthwise; scoop out insides*, leaving a ¼-inch-thick shell. Cut shells in half crosswise. Place shells on large baking sheet.

2. Preheat broiler. Combine 1 tablespoon Redhot® sauce and butter in small bowl; brush on inside of each potato shell. Broil shells, 6 inches from heat, 8 minutes or until golden brown and crispy.

3. Combine remaining 3 tablespoons Redhot® sauce with remaining ingredients in large bowl. Spoon about 1 tablespoon mixture into each potato shell. Broil 2 minutes or until cheese melts. Cut each piece in half to serve.                                          *Makes 12 servings*

*Reserve leftover potato for mashed potatoes, home-fries or soup.

**Prep Time:** 30 minutes
**Cook Time:** 1 hour 20 minutes

# GARLIC SKILLET POTATOES

❤ ❤ ❤

2 tablespoons vegetable or olive oil
4 large red potatoes, cut into thin wedges
½ cup chopped onion
1¼ teaspoons LAWRY'S® Garlic Powder with Parsley
¾ to 1 teaspoon LAWRY'S® Seasoned Salt
¾ teaspoon LAWRY'S® Seasoned Pepper
½ teaspoon sugar
Chopped fresh parsley (garnish)

In large skillet, heat oil; add potatoes, onion, Garlic Powder with Parsley, Seasoned Salt, Seasoned Pepper and sugar and cook, uncovered, over medium heat 25 to 30 minutes or until potatoes are tender and browned.

*Makes 4 to 6 servings*

**Serving Suggestion:** Sprinkle with chopped fresh parsley. Great served with steak, scrambled eggs or omelets.

*Grandma's Secret: Always store potatoes in a cool, dark and dry place. The ideal storage temperature is between 50°F to 55°F. Never refrigerate potatoes, because temperatures under 45°F will change potato starch to sugar, thus affecting their flavor and appearance.*

*Garlic Skillet Potatoes*

# PUFFY POTATOES

❤ ❤ ❤

4 slices bacon, diced
5 medium baking potatoes (about 3 pounds)
⅓ cup milk
¾ cup prepared HIDDEN VALLEY® Original Ranch® Salad
    Dressing & Recipe Mix
3 teaspoons chopped parsley, divided

Preheat oven to 400°F. In skillet, cook bacon until crisp; drain on paper towels. Crumble bacon and set aside. Pierce potatoes with fork; bake until tender, about 45 minutes. Cut slits lengthwise, then crosswise in top of each potato. Scoop out centers of potatoes and place in large bowl; reserve 4 potato skins. Mash potatoes. Add milk and salad dressing; beat until smooth. Stir in bacon and 2 teaspoons of the parsley. Fill skins with potato mixture. Bake at 400°F until puffy and golden, about 15 minutes. Sprinkle with remaining 1 teaspoon parsley.                    *Makes 4 servings*

**Note:** If desired, beat potatoes with ½ cup milk and bake in casserole dish instead of potato skins.

*Puffy Potatoes*

# POTATOES AND LEEKS AU GRATIN

♥ ♥ ♥

- 5 tablespoons butter or margarine, divided
- 2 large leeks, sliced
- 2 tablespoons minced garlic
- 2 pounds baking potatoes (about 4 medium), peeled
- 1 cup heavy cream
- 1 cup milk
- 3 eggs
- 2 teaspoons salt
- ¼ teaspoon ground white pepper
- 2 to 3 slices dense day-old white bread, such as French or Italian
- 2 ounces Parmesan cheese
  Fresh chives and salad burnet for garnish

1. Preheat oven to 375°F. Generously butter shallow oval 10-cup baking dish with 1 tablespoon butter; set aside.

2. Melt 2 tablespoons butter in large skillet over medium heat. Add leeks and garlic. Cook and stir 8 to 10 minutes until leeks are softened. Remove from heat; set aside.

*continued on page 190*

3. Cut potatoes crosswise into 1/16-inch-thick slices. Layer half of potato slices in prepared baking dish. Top with half of leek mixture. Repeat layers with remaining potato slices and leek mixture. Whisk together cream, milk, eggs, salt and pepper in medium bowl until well blended; pour evenly over leek mixture.

4. To prepare bread crumbs, tear bread slices into 1-inch pieces and place in food processor or blender; process until fine crumbs form. Measure 3/4 cup crumbs. Grate cheese into small bowl; stir in bread crumbs. Melt remaining 2 tablespoons butter in small saucepan; pour over crumbs, tossing to blend thoroughly. Sprinkle crumb mixture evenly over cream mixture.

5. Bake 50 to 60 minutes until top is golden and potatoes are tender. Let stand 5 to 10 minutes before serving. Garnish, if desired.

*Makes 6 to 8 servings*

*Grandma's Secret: Leeks are available all year, but are most plentiful from fall to early spring. In general, leeks are milder in flavor than other onions and garlic. The smaller the leek, the more tender it will be.*

# TOMATO SCALLOPED POTATOES

♥ ♥ ♥

1 can (14½ ounces) DEL MONTE® Diced Tomatoes
1 pound red potatoes, thinly sliced
1 medium onion, chopped
½ cup whipping cream
1 cup (4 ounces) shredded Swiss cheese
3 tablespoons grated Parmesan cheese

1. Preheat oven to 350°F.

2. Drain tomatoes, reserving liquid; pour liquid into measuring cup. Add water to measure 1 cup.

3. Add reserved liquid, potatoes and onion to large skillet; cover. Cook 10 minutes or until tender.

4. Place potato mixture in 1-quart baking dish; top with tomatoes and cream. Sprinkle with cheeses.

5. Bake 20 minutes or until hot and bubbly. Sprinkle with chopped parsley, if desired.

*Makes 6 servings*

**Prep Time:** 8 minutes
**Cook Time:** 30 minutes

# MASHED SWEET POTATOES & PARSNIPS

♥ ♥ ♥

2   large sweet potatoes (about 1¼ pounds), peeled and
        cut into 1-inch pieces
2   medium parsnips (about ½ pound), peeled and cut into
        ½-inch slices
¼   cup evaporated skimmed milk
1½  tablespoons butter or margarine
½   teaspoon salt
⅛   teaspoon nutmeg
¼   cup chopped chives or green onion tops

1. Combine sweet potatoes and parsnips in large saucepan. Cover with cold water and bring to a boil over high heat. Reduce heat; simmer uncovered 15 minutes or until vegetables are tender.

2. Drain vegetables and return to pan. Add milk, butter, salt and nutmeg. Mash potato mixture over low heat to desired consistency. Stir in chives.

*Makes 6 servings*

*Grandma's Secret: Parsnips are a pale white root vegetable similar to the carrot in shape. The parsnip, however, is broader at the top and has a smoother skin. The longer it stays in the ground, the sweeter it becomes.*

# RANCH PICNIC POTATO SALAD

❤ ❤ ❤

6   medium potatoes (about 3½ pounds), cooked, peeled
      and sliced
½   cup chopped celery
¼   cup sliced green onions
2   tablespoons chopped parsley
1   teaspoon salt
⅛   teaspoon black pepper
1   tablespoon Dijon-style mustard
1   cup prepared HIDDEN VALLEY® Original Ranch® Salad
      Dressing
2   hard-cooked eggs, finely chopped
      Paprika

In large bowl, combine potatoes, celery, onions, parsley, salt and pepper. In small bowl, stir mustard into salad dressing; pour over potato mixture and toss lightly. Cover and refrigerate several hours. Sprinkle with eggs and paprika. Serve in lettuce-lined bowl, if desired.     *Makes 8 servings*

*Ranch Picnic Potato Salad*

# Bounty of Breads

## ORANGE CHOCOLATE CHIP BREAD

♥ ♥ ♥

½ cup nonfat milk
½ cup plain nonfat yogurt
⅓ cup sugar
¼ cup orange juice
1 egg, slightly beaten
1 tablespoon freshly grated orange peel
3 cups all-purpose biscuit baking mix
½ cup HERSHEY'S MINI CHIPS® Semi-Sweet Chocolate

1. Heat oven to 350°F. Grease 9×5×3-inch loaf pan or spray with vegetable cooking spray. Stir together milk, yogurt, sugar, orange juice, egg and orange peel in large bowl; add baking mix. With spoon, beat until well blended, about 1 minute. Stir in small chocolate chips. Pour into prepared pan.

2. Bake 45 to 50 minutes or until wooden pick inserted in center comes out clean. Cool 10 minutes; remove from pan to wire rack. Cool completely before slicing. Garnish as desired. Wrap leftover bread in foil or plastic wrap. Store at room temperature or freeze for longer storage.

*Makes 1 loaf (16 slices)*

*Orange Chocolate Chip Bread*

# FARMER-STYLE SOUR CREAM BREAD

♥ ♥ ♥

1 cup sour cream, at room temperature
3 tablespoons water
2½ to 3 cups all-purpose flour, divided
1 package active dry yeast
2 tablespoons sugar
1½ teaspoons salt
¼ teaspoon baking soda
Vegetable oil or nonstick cooking spray
1 tablespoon poppy or sesame seeds

Stir together sour cream and water in small saucepan. Heat over low heat until temperature reaches 120° to 130°F. *Do not boil.* Combine 2 cups flour, yeast, sugar, salt and baking soda in a large bowl. Spread sour cream mixture evenly over flour mixture with rubber spatula. Stir until well blended. Turn out dough onto lightly floured surface. Knead 5 minutes or until smooth and elastic, gradually adding remaining flour to prevent sticking, if necessary.

Grease large baking sheet. Shape dough into ball; place on prepared sheet. Flatten into 8-inch circle. Brush with oil. Sprinkle with poppy seeds. Invert large bowl over dough and let rise in warm place 1 hour or until doubled in bulk.

Preheat oven to 350°F. Bake 22 to 27 minutes or until golden brown. Remove immediately from baking sheet. Cool completely on wire rack.

*Makes 8 to 12 servings*

*Farmer-Style Sour Cream Bread*

# CINNAMON HONEY BUNS

❤ ❤ ❤

3 tablespoons butter or margarine, softened and divided
½ cup honey, divided
¼ cup chopped toasted nuts
2 teaspoons ground cinnamon
1 loaf (1 pound) frozen bread dough, thawed according
    to package directions
⅔ cup raisins

Grease 12 muffin cups with 1 tablespoon butter. To prepare honey-nut topping, mix together 1 tablespoon butter, ¼ cup honey and chopped nuts. Place 1 teaspoon topping in each muffin cup. To prepare filling, mix together remaining 2 tablespoons butter, remaining ¼ cup honey and cinnamon. Roll out bread dough onto floured surface into 18×8-inch rectangle. Spread filling evenly over dough. Sprinkle with raisins. Starting with long side, roll dough into log. Cut log into 12 (1½-inch) slices. Place 1 slice, cut-side up, into each prepared muffin cup. Set muffin pan in warm place; let dough rise 30 minutes. Place muffin pan on foil-lined baking sheet. Bake at 375°F 20 minutes or until buns are golden brown. Remove from oven; cool in pan 5 minutes. Invert muffin pan to remove buns. *Makes 12 buns*

*Favorite recipe from* **National Honey Board**

*Cinnamon Honey Buns*

# PEACHY OAT BRAN MUFFINS

♥ ♥ ♥

1½ cups oat bran
½ cup all-purpose flour
⅓ cup firmly packed brown sugar
2 teaspoons baking powder
1 teaspoon cinnamon
½ teaspoon salt
¾ cup lowfat milk
1 egg, beaten
¼ cup vegetable oil
1 can (15 ounces) DEL MONTE® LITE® Yellow Cling
   Sliced Peaches, drained and chopped
⅓ cup chopped walnuts

1. Preheat oven to 425°F. Combine oat bran, flour, brown sugar, baking powder, cinnamon and salt; mix well.

2. Combine milk, egg and oil. Add to dry ingredients; stir just enough to blend. Fold in fruit and nuts.

3. Fill greased muffin cups with batter. Sprinkle with granulated sugar, if desired.

4. Bake 20 to 25 minutes or until golden brown.

*Makes 12 medium muffins*

**Prep Time:** 10 minutes
**Cook Time:** 25 minutes

# DOWNHOME CORNSTICKS

❤ ❤ ❤

⅔ cup yellow or blue cornmeal
⅓ cup all-purpose flour
3 tablespoons sugar
1½ teaspoons baking powder
½ teaspoon LAWRY'S® Seasoned Salt
1 cup milk
2 tablespoons melted butter
1 egg, well beaten
2 tablespoons diced green chiles

In medium bowl, combine cornmeal, flour, sugar, baking powder and Seasoned Salt. Add in mixture of milk, butter and egg; blend well. Add chiles. Spoon batter into lightly greased corn shaped molds. Bake in 425°F. oven on lowest rack 20 to 25 minutes.               *Makes 12 cornsticks*

**Presentation:** Serve warm with whipped honey butter.

*Grandma's Secret:* These spicy bread sticks are a nice complement to any Southwestern or Tex-Mex dinner. To add some color and variety to the bread basket, make half of the recipe with yellow cornmeal and the other half with blue cornmeal.

# FREEZER BUTTERMILK BISCUITS

♥ ♥ ♥

                3  cups all-purpose flour
                1  tablespoon baking powder
                1  tablespoon sugar
                1  teaspoon baking soda
                ½  teaspoon salt
                ⅔  cup shortening
                1  cup buttermilk*

*You can substitute soured fresh milk. To sour milk, place 1 tablespoon lemon juice plus enough milk to equal 1 cup in 2-cup measure. Stir; let stand 5 minutes before using.

Combine flour, baking powder, sugar, baking soda and salt in large bowl. Cut in shortening with pastry blender or 2 knives until mixture resembles fine crumbs. Stir buttermilk into flour mixture until mixture forms soft dough that leaves side of bowl.

Turn out dough onto well-floured surface. Knead 10 times; roll into 8-inch square. Cut dough into 16 (2-inch) squares.** Place squares on baking sheet lined with plastic wrap. Freeze about 3 hours or until firm. Remove squares and place in airtight freezer container. Freeze up to 1 month.

When ready to prepare, preheat oven to 400°F. Place frozen squares 1½ inches apart on ungreased baking sheets. Bake 20 to 25 minutes or until golden brown. Serve warm.                                    *Makes 16 biscuits*

**To bake immediately, preheat oven to 450°F. Place squares 1½ inches apart on ungreased baking sheets. Bake 10 to 12 minutes or until golden brown. Serve warm.

*Freezer Buttermilk Biscuits*

# BREADSTICK SAMPLER

♥ ♥ ♥

1 can (11 ounces) breadstick dough (8 breadsticks)
1 tablespoon grated Parmesan cheese
⅛ teaspoon ground red pepper
½ teaspoon dried basil leaves
½ teaspoon dried oregano leaves
½ teaspoon dried thyme leaves
2 tablespoons olive oil
1 tablespoon garlic powder, divided

1. Preheat oven to 350°F. Separate and unroll strips of dough. Twist each breadstick several times and place on greased cookie sheet about 1 inch apart. Press ends firmly onto pans to anchor.

2. Combine cheese and pepper in small bowl. Combine basil, oregano and thyme in another small bowl.

3. Brush breadsticks with olive oil. For garlic breadsticks, sprinkle 2 breadsticks each with 1 teaspoon garlic powder. For cheese breadsticks, sprinkle 2 breadsticks each with 1 teaspoon cheese mixture. For herb breadsticks, sprinkle 2 breadsticks each with ½ teaspoon basil mixture. For garlic-cheese-herb breadsticks, sprinkle remaining 2 breadsticks each with remaining 1 teaspoon garlic, 1 teaspoon cheese mixture and ½ teaspoon basil mixture.

4. Bake 15 minutes or until golden brown. Transfer to wire rack to cool 5 minutes. Serve warm.                    *Makes 8 breadsticks*

*Breadstick Sampler*

# SAVORY SUMMERTIME OATBREAD

♥ ♥ ♥

Nonstick cooking spray
½ cup finely chopped onion
2 cups whole wheat flour
4¼ to 4½ cups all-purpose flour, divided
2 cups uncooked rolled oats
¼ cup sugar
2 packages quick-rising active dry yeast
1½ teaspoons salt
1½ cups water
1¼ cups skim milk
¼ cup butter
1 cup finely shredded carrots
3 tablespoons dried parsley leaves
1 tablespoon butter, melted

1. Spray small skillet with cooking spray; heat over medium heat until hot. Cook and stir onion 3 minutes or until tender. Set aside.

2. Combine whole wheat flour, 1 cup all-purpose flour, oats, sugar, yeast and salt in large mixer bowl. Mix on low speed for 30 seconds or until well blended.

*continued on page 210*

*Savory Summertime Oatbread*

*Savory Summertime Oatbread, continued*

3. Combine water, milk and ¼ cup butter in medium saucepan. Heat over low heat until mixture reaches 120° to 130°F.* Add to flour mixture. Blend at low speed just until dry ingredients are moistened; beat 3 minutes at medium speed.

4. Stir in carrots, onion and parsley and remaining 3¼ to 3½ cups all-purpose flour until dough is no longer sticky.

5. Knead dough on lightly floured surface 5 to 8 minutes or until dough is smooth and elastic. Shape into ball; place in large bowl lightly sprayed with nonstick cooking spray. Turn dough once to coat surface with cooking spray. Cover and let rise in warm place about 30 minutes or until doubled in bulk.

6. Spray two 8×4-inch loaf pans with nonstick cooking spray. Punch dough down. Cover and let rest 10 minutes. Shape dough into 2 loaves; place in prepared pans. Brush lightly with melted butter.

7. Cover; let rise in warm place 30 minutes or until doubled in bulk. Meanwhile, preheat oven to 350°F.

8. Bake 40 to 45 minutes or until bread sounds hollow when tapped. Remove from pans immediately; cool on wire racks.      *Makes 2 loaves (24 slices)*

*Too much heat will kill the yeast.

# PINEAPPLE-RAISIN MUFFINS

♥ ♥ ♥

¼ cup finely chopped pecans
¼ cup packed light brown sugar
2 cups all-purpose flour
¼ cup granulated sugar
2½ teaspoons baking powder
¾ teaspoon salt
½ teaspoon ground cinnamon
6 tablespoons cold butter
½ cup raisins
1 can (8 ounces) crushed pineapple in juice, undrained
⅓ cup unsweetened pineapple juice
1 egg

1. Preheat oven to 400°F. Paper-line or grease 12 (2½-inch) muffin cups.

2. Combine pecans and brown sugar in small bowl; set aside. Combine flour, granulated sugar, baking powder, salt and cinnamon in large bowl. Cut in butter with pastry blender or 2 knives until mixture resembles fine crumbs. Stir in raisins.

3. Combine undrained pineapple, pineapple juice and egg in small bowl until blended; stir into flour mixture just until moistened. Spoon evenly into prepared muffin cups, filling ⅔ full. Sprinkle with pecan mixture.

4. Bake 20 to 25 minutes or until golden brown and toothpick inserted in center comes out clean. Immediately remove from pan; cool on wire rack 10 minutes. Serve warm or cold. *Makes 12 muffins*

# WHOLE WHEAT HERB BREAD

❤ ❤ ❤

⅔ cup water
⅔ cup fat-free (skim) milk
2 teaspoons sugar
2 envelopes active dry yeast
3 egg whites, lightly beaten
3 tablespoons olive oil
1 teaspoon salt
½ teaspoon dried basil leaves
½ teaspoon dried oregano leaves
4 to 4½ cups whole wheat flour

1. Bring water to a boil in small saucepan. Remove from heat; stir in milk and sugar. When mixture is warm (110° to 115°F), add yeast. Mix well; let stand 10 minutes or until bubbly.

2. Combine egg whites, oil, salt, basil and oregano in large bowl until well blended. Add yeast mixture; mix well. Add 4 cups flour, ½ cup at a time, mixing well after each addition, until dough is no longer sticky. Knead about 5 minutes or until smooth and elastic, adding more flour if dough is sticky. Form into a ball. Cover and let rise in warm place about 1 hour or until doubled in bulk.

3. Preheat oven to 350°F. Punch dough down and place on lightly floured surface. Divide into 4 pieces and roll each piece into a ball. Lightly spray baking sheet with nonstick cooking spray. Place dough balls on prepared baking sheet. Bake 30 to 35 minutes or until golden brown and loaves sound hollow when tapped with finger.

*Makes 24 slices*

*Whole Wheat Herb Bread*

# THYME-CHEESE BUBBLE LOAF

♥ ♥ ♥

1 package active dry yeast
1 teaspoon sugar
1 cup warm water
3 cups all-purpose flour
1 teaspoon salt
2 tablespoons vegetable oil
1 cup (4 ounces) shredded Monterey Jack cheese
4 tablespoons butter or margarine, melted
¼ cup chopped parsley
3 teaspoons finely chopped fresh thyme *or* ¾ teaspoon dried thyme leaves

1. Sprinkle yeast and sugar over warm water (105°-115°F) in small bowl; stir until yeast is dissolved. Let stand 5 minutes or until mixture is bubbly.

2. Combine flour and salt in food processor. With food processor running, add yeast mixture and oil. Process until mixture forms dough that leaves side of bowl. If dough is too dry, add 1 to 2 tablespoons water. If dough is too wet, add 1 to 2 tablespoons additional flour until dough leaves side of bowl. Dough will be sticky.

3. Place dough in large greased bowl. Turn dough over so that top is greased. Cover with towel; let rise in warm place about 1 hour or until doubled in bulk.

*continued on page 216*

*Thyme-Cheese Bubble Loaf*

*Thyme-Cheese Bubble Loaf, continued*

4. Punch down dough. Knead cheese into dough on lightly floured surface until evenly distributed. Cover with towel; let rest 10 minutes.

5. Grease 1½-quart casserole dish or 8½×4½-inch loaf pan; set aside. Combine butter, parsley and thyme in small bowl.

6. Roll out dough into 8×6-inch rectangle with lightly floured rolling pin. Cut dough into 48 (1-inch) squares with pizza cutter. Shape each square into a ball. Dip into parsley mixture. Place in prepared pan.

7. Cover with towel; let rise in warm place about 45 minutes or until doubled in bulk. Preheat oven to 375°F.

8. Bake 35 to 40 minutes or until top is golden and loaf sounds hollow when tapped. Immediately remove from casserole dish; cool on wire rack 30 minutes. Serve warm. Store leftover bread in refrigerator.      *Makes 1 loaf*

*Grandma's Secret: Thyme had a reputation as a medicinal herb, thought to relieve epilepsy, melancholy, hangovers and a variety of nervous disorders. The essential oil in Thyme was even used as a battlefield antiseptic as recently as World War I.*

# BACON BRUNCH BUNS

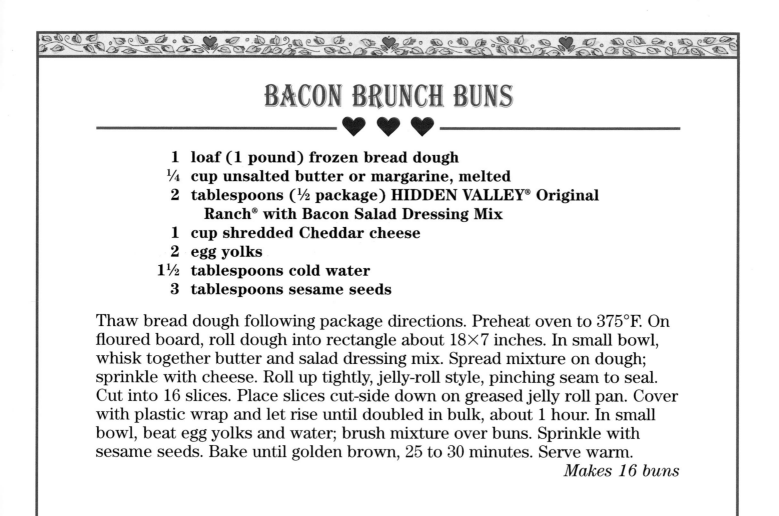

♥ ♥ ♥

 1  loaf (1 pound) frozen bread dough
¼  cup unsalted butter or margarine, melted
 2  tablespoons (½ package) HIDDEN VALLEY® Original
       Ranch® with Bacon Salad Dressing Mix
 1  cup shredded Cheddar cheese
 2  egg yolks
1½  tablespoons cold water
 3  tablespoons sesame seeds

Thaw bread dough following package directions. Preheat oven to 375°F. On floured board, roll dough into rectangle about 18×7 inches. In small bowl, whisk together butter and salad dressing mix. Spread mixture on dough; sprinkle with cheese. Roll up tightly, jelly-roll style, pinching seam to seal. Cut into 16 slices. Place slices cut-side down on greased jelly roll pan. Cover with plastic wrap and let rise until doubled in bulk, about 1 hour. In small bowl, beat egg yolks and water; brush mixture over buns. Sprinkle with sesame seeds. Bake until golden brown, 25 to 30 minutes. Serve warm.

*Makes 16 buns*

# OATMEAL-RAISIN BREAD

♥ ♥ ♥

### 1½-POUND LOAF INGREDIENTS

1¼ cups water
¼ cup nonfat dry milk
2 tablespoons honey
1 tablespoon butter or margarine
1½ teaspoons salt
3 cups bread flour
1½ teaspoons rapid-rise yeast
½ cup old-fashioned oats
½ cup raisins

## BREAD MACHINE DIRECTIONS

1. Measure carefully, placing all ingredients except oats and raisins in bread machine pan in order specified by owner's manual.

2. Program basic cycle and desired crust setting; press start. Add oats and raisins at the beep or at the end of first kneading cycle. Remove baked bread from pan; cool on wire rack.          *Makes 12 or 16 servings*

*Oatmeal-Raisin Bread*

# CHEESY HAM AND PEPPER MUFFINS

♥ ♥ ♥

2½ cups all-purpose flour
3 tablespoons sugar
1 tablespoon baking powder
¼ teaspoon ground black pepper
1 cup milk
6 tablespoons vegetable oil
2 eggs, beaten
2 tablespoons Dijon mustard
¾ cup shredded Swiss cheese
¾ cup diced cooked ham
3 tablespoons chopped red or green bell pepper

Preheat oven to 400°F. Grease or paper-line 12 (2½-inch) muffin cups.

Combine flour, sugar, baking powder and black pepper in large bowl. Whisk together milk, oil, eggs and mustard in small bowl until blended. Stir into flour mixture just until moistened. Fold in cheese, ham and bell pepper. Spoon evenly into prepared muffin cups.

Bake 19 to 21 minutes or until toothpick inserted into centers comes out clean. Cool in muffin pan on wire rack 5 minutes. Remove from pan and cool on wire rack 10 minutes.                                        *Makes 12 muffins*

*Cheesy Ham and Pepper Muffins*

# SOUTHERN CARAMEL PECAN ROLLS

♥ ♥ ♥

**TOPPING**

- ⅔ cup sifted powdered sugar
- ⅔ cup dark brown sugar
- ½ cup whipping cream
- 1 teaspoon vanilla
  WESSON® No-Stick Cooking Spray
- 1 cup coarsely chopped pecans

**ROLLS**

- 1 cup dark raisins
- ⅓ cup brandy
- 2 (1-pound) loaves frozen sweet or white bread dough, thawed, but not doubled in size
- ¼ cup WESSON® Best Blend Oil
- ½ cup packed dark brown sugar
- 1 tablespoon ground cinnamon
- ½ teaspoon ground nutmeg

## TOPPING

In a medium bowl, stir together sugars, whipping cream and vanilla. Spray two 9×1½-inch round cake pans with Wesson® Cooking Spray. Evenly divide mixture between pans and sprinkle with pecans; set aside pans.

*continued on page 224*

*Southern Caramel Pecan Rolls*

*Southern Caramel Pecan Rolls, continued*

## ROLLS
In a small bowl, soak raisins in brandy for 30 minutes; set aside and stir occasionally.

On floured surface, roll *each* loaf into 12×8×¼-inch rectangle. Generously brush *each* sheet of dough with Wesson® Oil. In a small bowl, mix together sugar, cinnamon and nutmeg. Sprinkle over dough; top with soaked raisins. Roll up rectangles jelly-roll style starting with long edge. Pinch dough to seal. Cut into 12 slices. Place rolls, spiral side down, in cake pans. Cover with towels and let rise in warm place for 30 minutes or until nearly double in size. Preheat oven to 375°F. Bake, uncovered, for 15 to 20 minutes. Cover pans with foil to prevent overbrowning and bake an additional 10 minutes. Cool in pans 7 minutes. Invert onto serving plate. Best when served warm.

*Makes 24 rolls*

# ORANGE BREAKFAST LOAF

♥ ♥ ♥

**1½-POUND LOAF INGREDIENTS**

- 1 **cup water**
- 1 **teaspoon salt**
- ⅓ **cup orange juice**
- 2 **tablespoons vegetable oil**
- 2 **tablespoons sugar**
- 1 **cup oats**
- 1 **cup whole wheat flour**
- 2 **cups all-purpose flour**
- 1 **teaspoon grated orange peel**
- ½ **cup dried cranberries**
- 2 **teaspoons active dry yeast**

## BREAD MACHINE INSTRUCTIONS

1. Measure carefully, placing all ingredients in bread machine pan in order specified by owner's manual.

2. Program basic or white cycle and desired crust setting; press start. Remove baked bread from pan; cool on wire rack.

*Makes 1 (1½-pound) loaf (12 to 16 servings)*

# CRUSTY RYE BREAD

♥ ♥ ♥

### 1½-POUND LOAF INGREDIENTS

- 1 cup water
- 1 teaspoon salt
- 1 tablespoon butter or margarine, softened
- 2½ cups all-purpose flour
- ½ cup rye flour
- ¼ cup packed light brown sugar
- 3 strips pared orange peel, chopped
- 1 teaspoon caraway seeds
- 2 teaspoons active dry yeast

### BREAD MACHINE INSTRUCTIONS

1. Measure carefully, placing all ingredients in bread machine pan in order specified by owner's manual.

2. Program basic or white cycle and desired crust setting; press start. Remove baked bread from pan; cool on wire rack.

*Makes 1 (1½-pound) loaf (12 to 16 servings)*

*Crusty Rye Bread*

# SOUTHERN SPOON BREAD

♥ ♥ ♥

4 eggs, separated
3 cups milk
1 cup yellow cornmeal
3 tablespoons butter or margarine
1 teaspoon salt
¼ teaspoon ground black pepper *or* ⅛ teaspoon ground
     red pepper
1 teaspoon baking powder
1 tablespoon grated Parmesan cheese (optional)

Preheat oven to 375°F. Spray 2-quart round casserole with nonstick cooking spray; set aside. Beat egg yolks in small bowl; set aside.

Heat milk almost to a boil in medium saucepan over medium heat. Gradually beat in cornmeal using wire whisk. Cook 2 minutes, stirring constantly. Whisk in butter, salt and pepper. Beat about ¼ cup cornmeal mixture into egg yolks. Beat egg yolk mixture into remaining cornmeal mixture; set aside.

Beat egg whites in large bowl with electric mixer at high speed until stiff peaks form. Stir baking powder into cornmeal mixture. Stir about ¼ cup egg whites into cornmeal mixture. Gradually fold in remaining egg whites. Pour into prepared casserole; sprinkle with cheese, if desired.

Bake 30 to 35 minutes or until golden brown and toothpick inserted into center comes out clean. Serve immediately.               *Makes 6 servings*

*Southern Spoon Bread*

# CHIVE WHOLE WHEAT DROP BISCUITS

❤ ❤ ❤

1¼ cups whole wheat flour
¾ cup all-purpose flour
3 tablespoons toasted wheat germ, divided
1 tablespoon baking powder
1 tablespoon chopped fresh chives *or* 1 teaspoon dried chives
2 teaspoons sugar
3 tablespoons butter
1 cup fat-free (skim) milk
½ cup shredded low-fat process American cheese

1. Preheat oven to 450°F. Spray baking sheet with nonstick cooking spray. Combine whole wheat flour, all-purpose flour, 2 tablespoons wheat germ, baking powder, chives and sugar in medium bowl. Cut in butter with pastry blender or 2 knives until mixture resembles coarse meal. Add milk and American cheese; stir until just combined.

2. Drop dough by rounded teaspoonfuls onto prepared baking sheet about 1 inch apart. Sprinkle with remaining 1 tablespoon wheat germ. Bake 10 to 12 minutes or until golden brown. Remove immediately from baking sheet. Serve warm.

*Makes 12 servings*

# HONEY MUFFINS

♥ ♥ ♥

1 can (8 ounces) DOLE® Crushed Pineapple in Juice
1½ cups wheat bran cereal (not flakes)
⅔ cup buttermilk
1 egg, slightly beaten
⅓ cup chopped pecans or walnuts
3 tablespoons vegetable oil
½ cup honey, divided
⅔ cup whole wheat flour
½ teaspoon baking soda
⅛ teaspoon salt

Combine undrained pineapple, cereal and buttermilk in large bowl. Let stand 10 minutes until cereal has absorbed liquid. Stir in egg, pecans, oil and ¼ cup honey. Combine flour, baking soda and salt in small bowl. Stir into bran mixture until just moistened. Spoon batter into prepared cups, filling to the top.

Microwave at HIGH (100%) for 3½ to 4 minutes, rotating pan ½ turn after 1½ minutes. Muffins are done when they look dry and set on top. Remove from oven; immediately spoon 1 teaspoon of remaining honey over each muffin. Remove to cooling rack after honey has been absorbed. Repeat procedure with remaining batter and honey. Serve warm.

*Makes 12 muffins*

**Microwave Directions:** Line six microwavable muffin cups or six 6-ounce microwavable custard cups with double thickness paper baking cups. (Outer cup will absorb moisture so inner cup sticks to cooked muffin.)

# WALNUT CHEDDAR APPLE BREAD

♥ ♥ ♥

½ cup butter, softened
1 cup packed light brown sugar
2 eggs
1 teaspoon vanilla
2 cups all-purpose flour
2 teaspoons baking powder
1 teaspoon baking soda
¼ teaspoon salt
1 cup sour cream
¼ cup milk
1 cup (4 ounces) shredded Cheddar cheese
1 cup diced dried apple
½ cup coarsely chopped walnuts

Preheat oven to 350°F. Grease 9×5-inch loaf pan. Beat butter and sugar in large bowl with electric mixer on medium speed until light and fluffy. Beat in eggs and vanilla until blended. Combine flour, baking powder, baking soda and salt in small bowl. Add flour mixture to butter mixture on low speed alternately with sour cream and milk, beginning and ending with flour mixture. Mix well after each addition. Stir in cheese, apple and walnuts on low speed until blended. Spoon into prepared pan.

Bake 50 to 55 minutes or until toothpick inserted in center comes out clean. Cool in pan 15 minutes. Remove from pan and cool completely on wire rack. Store tightly wrapped in plastic wrap at room temperature.

*Makes 1 loaf*

*Walnut Cheddar Apple Bread*

# JALAPEÑO CORN BREAD

❤ ❤ ❤

## 1½-POUND LOAF INGREDIENTS

- ¾ cup plus 1 tablespoon water
- 1 cup thawed frozen or drained canned corn
- 1 tablespoon buttermilk powder
- 1 tablespoon minced drained bottled jalapeño peppers*
- 1½ teaspoons salt
- 1 tablespoon sugar
- ¾ cup cornmeal
- 2¾ cups bread flour
- 1 cup shredded Monterey Jack cheese
- 1 teaspoon rapid-rise yeast

*For less spicy bread, use 1 to 2 teaspoons jalapeño peppers. Jalapeño peppers can sting and irritate the skin; wear rubber gloves when handling peppers and do not touch eyes.

## BREAD MACHINE DIRECTIONS

1. Measure carefully, placing all ingredients in bread machine pan in order specified by owner's manual.

2. Program basic or white cycle and desired crust setting; press start. Remove baked bread from pan; cool on wire rack.

*Makes 12 or 16 servings*

*Jalapeño Corn Bread*

# FOCCACIA

1 (1-pound) loaf frozen bread dough
1½ tablespoons olive oil
½ cup finely shredded Mozzarella cheese
1 teaspoon dried rosemary
1 teaspoon LAWRY'S® Garlic Powder with Parsley
½ teaspoon dried oregano, crushed

Preheat oven to 375°F. On a lightly floured surface roll thawed loaf into a 9×13 inch rectangle. If dough shrinks back after rolling, let the dough rest for a few minutes then continue rolling to correct size. Transfer dough to a greased 9×13 inch baking pan. Brush with olive oil. Let rise about 30 to 60 minutes. Pressing down dough with finger tips to make dimples in dough. Sprinkle with cheese and spices. Bake 15 to 20 minutes or until golden brown. Remove from pan to cool on wire rack. *Makes 8 servings*

**Presentation:** Slice in strips or squares for serving.

# HERB BISCUITS

♥ ♥ ♥

¼ cup hot water (130°F)
1½ teaspoons (½ package) fast-rising active dry yeast
2½ cups all-purpose flour
3 tablespoons sugar
1½ teaspoons baking powder
½ teaspoon baking soda
½ teaspoon salt
5 tablespoons cold butter, cut into pieces
2 teaspoons finely chopped fresh parsley *or* ½ teaspoon dried parsley flakes
2 teaspoons finely chopped fresh basil *or* ½ teaspoon dried basil leaves
2 teaspoons finely chopped fresh chives *or* ½ teaspoon dried chives
¾ cup buttermilk

1. Preheat oven to 425°F. Spray cookie sheet with nonstick cooking spray. Combine hot water and yeast in small cup; let stand 2 to 3 minutes. Combine flour, sugar, baking powder, baking soda and salt in medium bowl; cut in butter using pastry blender or 2 knives until mixture resembles coarse crumbs. Mix in parsley, basil and chives. Stir in buttermilk and yeast mixture to make soft dough. Turn dough out onto lightly floured surface. Knead 15 to 20 times.

2. Roll to ½-inch thickness. Cut hearts or other shapes with 2½-inch cookie cutter. Place biscuits on prepared cookie sheet. Bake 12 to 15 minutes or until browned. Cool on wire racks. Serve immediately. *Makes 18 biscuits*

# IRISH SODA BREAD

♥ ♥ ♥

- 4 cups all-purpose flour
- ¼ cup sugar
- 1 tablespoon baking powder
- 1 teaspoon baking soda
- 1 teaspoon salt
- 1 tablespoon caraway seeds
- ⅓ cup vegetable shortening
- 1 cup raisins or currants
- 1 egg
- 1¾ cups buttermilk

1. Preheat oven to 350°F. Grease large baking sheet; set aside. Sift flour, sugar, baking powder, baking soda and salt into large bowl. Stir in caraway seeds. Cut in shortening with pastry blender or 2 knives until mixture resembles coarse crumbs. Stir in raisins. Beat egg in medium bowl using fork. Add buttermilk; beat until well combined. Add buttermilk mixture to flour mixture; stir until mixture forms soft dough that clings together and forms a ball.

2. Turn dough out onto well-floured surface. Knead dough gently 10 to 12 times. Place dough on prepared baking sheet. Pat dough into 7-inch round. Score top of dough with tip of sharp knife, making an "x" about 4 inches long and ¼ inch deep.

3. Bake 55 to 60 minutes or until toothpick inserted in center comes out clean. Immediately remove from baking sheet; cool on wire rack. Bread is best eaten the day it is made.  *Makes 12 servings*

*Irish Soda Bread*

# HONEY WHEAT BROWN-AND-SERVE ROLLS

❤ ❤ ❤

       2   packages active dry yeast
       1   teaspoon sugar
       ¾   cup warm water (105° to 115°F)
       2   cups whole wheat flour
       2   to 3 cups all-purpose flour, divided
       ¼   cup vegetable shortening
       ¼   cup honey
       1   teaspoon salt
       1   egg

1. Sprinkle yeast and sugar over warm water in small bowl; stir until yeast is dissolved. Let stand 5 minutes until mixture is bubbly. Combine whole wheat flour and 2 cups all-purpose flour in medium bowl. Measure 1½ cups flour mixture into large bowl. Add yeast mixture, shortening, honey, salt and egg. Beat with electric mixer at low speed until smooth. Increase mixer speed to medium; beat 2 minutes. Reduce speed to low; beat in 1 cup flour mixture. Increase mixer speed to medium; beat 2 minutes. Stir in remaining flour mixture and enough additional all-purpose flour (about ¼ cup) with wooden spoon to make a soft dough.

2. Turn dough out onto lightly floured surface. Knead 8 to 10 minutes or until smooth and elastic, adding more flour to prevent sticking, if necessary. Shape dough into a ball; place in large greased bowl. Turn once to grease surface. Cover with clean kitchen towel. Let rise in warm place (80° to 85°F) about 1½ hours or until doubled in bulk.

*continued on page 242*

*Honey Wheat Brown-and-Serve Rolls*

*Honey Wheat Brown-and-Serve Rolls, continued*

3. Punch down dough. Turn dough onto lightly floured surface. Knead dough briefly; cover and let rest 15 minutes. Meanwhile, grease 24 muffin cups.

4. Divide dough into 24 pieces. Cut 1 piece into thirds. Roll each third into a ball. Place 3 balls in each muffin cup. Repeat with remaining dough. Cover and let rise in warm place about 30 minutes until doubled in bulk.

5. Preheat oven to 275°F.* Bake 20 to 25 minutes or until rolls are set but not brown. Immediately remove rolls from muffin cups and cool completely on wire racks. Store in resealable plastic food storage bags in refrigerator or freezer.

6. To bake rolls, thaw rolls if frozen. Preheat oven to 400°F. Grease large jelly-roll pan. Place rolls on jelly-roll pan. Bake 8 to 10 minutes or until golden brown.

*Makes 24 rolls*

*To bake rolls immediately, preheat oven to 375°F. Bake 15 to 20 minutes or until golden brown. Immediately remove from pan. Serve warm.

*Grandma's Secret: One package of yeast contains thousands of microscopic living plants that are activated by warm liquid and fed by sugar and starch. Yeast releases carbon dioxide gas bubbles that become trapped in the gluten network, causing doughs and batters to rise.*

# BUTTERMILK OATMEAL SCONES

♥ ♥ ♥

2 cups all-purpose flour, sifted
1 cup uncooked rolled oats
⅓ cup granulated sugar
1 tablespoon baking powder
½ teaspoon baking soda
⅛ teaspoon salt
6 tablespoons cold unsalted margarine, cut into small pieces
1 cup buttermilk

Preheat oven to 375°F. Grease baking sheets; set aside.

Combine flour, oats, sugar, baking powder, baking soda and salt in large bowl. Cut in margarine with pastry blender or process in food processor until mixture resembles coarse crumbs. Add buttermilk; stir with fork until soft dough forms. Turn out dough onto lightly floured surface; knead 10 to 12 times. Roll out dough to ½-inch-thick rectangle with lightly floured rolling pin. Cut dough into circles with lightly floured 1½-inch biscuit cutter. Place on prepared baking sheets. Brush tops with buttermilk and sprinkle with sugar. Bake 18 to 20 minutes or until golden brown and wooden pick inserted in center comes out clean. Remove from baking sheets. Cool on wire racks 10 minutes. Serve warm or cool completely.

*Makes about 30 scones*

*Favorite recipe from* **The Sugar Association, Inc.**

# Cakes & Cookies

## BANANA-NUT CAKE

♥ ♥ ♥

2¼ cups all-purpose flour
¾ cup uncooked rolled oats
2 teaspoons ground cinnamon
2 teaspoons baking powder
1 teaspoon baking soda
¼ teaspoon salt
2 cups mashed ripe bananas (about 6 medium bananas)
¾ cup thawed frozen unsweetened apple juice concentrate
4 eggs, beaten
½ cup butter or margarine, melted
2 teaspoons vanilla
¾ cup chopped walnuts
Cream Cheese Glaze (page 246)

Preheat oven to 350°F. Combine dry ingredients in large bowl. Add all remaining ingredients *except* walnuts and Cream Cheese Glaze; mix well.

*continued on page 246*

*Banana-Nut Cake*

*Banana-Nut Cake, continued*

Stir in walnuts; spread into well-greased Bundt or tube pan. Bake 50 to 55 minutes or until toothpick inserted in center comes out clean. Cool in pan on wire rack 15 minutes; turn cake out onto wire rack. Cool completely. Prepare Cream Cheese Glaze. Spoon over top of cake, letting excess glaze drip down sides. Serve at room temperature or chilled.

*Makes 12 servings*

## CREAM CHEESE GLAZE

1   package (3 ounces) cream cheese, softened
2   tablespoons thawed frozen unsweetened apple juice
       concentrate
¼   teaspoon vanilla
⅛   teaspoon ground cinnamon

Combine all ingredients in small bowl; beat until smooth.

# DOUBLE CHOCOLATE CREAM CAKE

### ♥ ♥ ♥

1   package **DUNCAN HINES®** Moist Deluxe Butter Recipe
      Fudge Cake Mix
1   envelope whipped topping mix
½   cup chocolate syrup
      Maraschino cherries with stems for garnish

Preheat oven to 375°F. Grease and flour 13×9-inch pan.

Prepare, bake and cool cake as directed on package.

Prepare whipped topping mix as directed on package. Fold in chocolate syrup until blended. Refrigerate until ready to serve.

To serve, spoon topping over cake slices. Garnish with maraschino cherries.

*Makes 12 to 16 servings*

**Tip:** For best consistency, chill chocolate syrup before using.

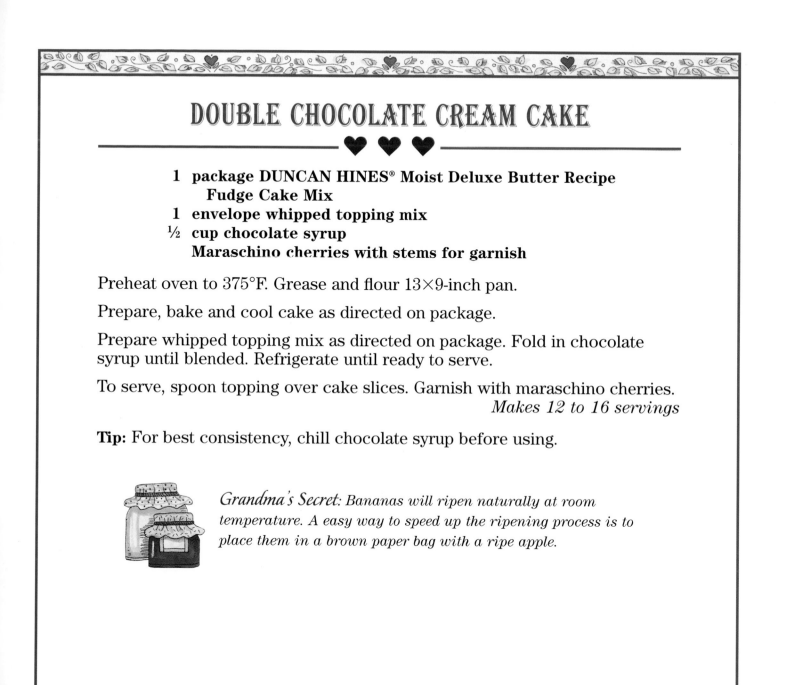

*Grandma's Secret: Bananas will ripen naturally at room temperature. A easy way to speed up the ripening process is to place them in a brown paper bag with a ripe apple.*

# ELEGANT CHOCOLATE ANGEL TORTE

♥ ♥ ♥

⅓ cup **HERSHEY'S Cocoa**
1 package (about 15 ounces) "two-step" angel food cake
   mix
2 envelopes (1.3 ounces each) dry whipped topping mix
1 cup cold nonfat milk
1 teaspoon vanilla extract
1 cup strawberry purée*
   **Strawberries**

*Mash 2 cups sliced fresh strawberries (or frozen berries, thawed) in blender or food processor. Cover; blend until smooth. Purée should measure 1 cup.

1. Move oven rack to lowest position.

2. Sift cocoa over contents of cake flour packet; stir to blend. Proceed with mixing cake as directed on package. Bake and cool as directed for 10-inch tube pan. Carefully run knife along side of pan to loosen cake; remove from pan. Using serrated knife, slice cake horizontally into four layers.

3. Prepare whipped topping mix as directed on package, using 1 cup nonfat milk and 1 teaspoon vanilla. Blend in strawberry purée.

4. Place bottom cake layer on serving plate; spread with ¼ of topping. Set next cake layer on top; spread with ¼ of topping. Continue layering cake and topping. Garnish with strawberries. Refrigerate until ready to serve. Slice cake with sharp serrated knife, cutting with gentle sawing motion. Cover; refrigerate leftover cake.                    *Makes about 16 servings*

*Elegant Chocolate Angel Torte*

# MOM'S FAVORITE WHITE CAKE

♥ ♥ ♥

2¼ cups cake flour
1 tablespoon baking powder
½ teaspoon salt
½ cup butter or margarine, softened
1½ cups sugar
4 egg whites
2 teaspoons vanilla
1 cup milk
Strawberry Frosting (page 252)
Fruit Filling (page 252)
Fresh strawberries (optional)

Preheat oven to 350°F. Line bottoms of two 9-inch round cake pans with waxed paper; lightly grease paper. Combine flour, baking powder and salt in medium bowl; set aside.

Beat butter and sugar in large bowl with electric mixer at medium speed until light and fluffy. Add egg whites, two at a time, beating well after each addition. Add vanilla; beat until blended. Add flour mixture alternately with milk, beating well after each addition. Pour batter evenly into prepared pans.

Bake 25 minutes or until toothpick inserted into centers comes out clean. Cool layers in pans on wire rack 10 minutes. Loosen edges and invert layers onto rack to cool completely.

*continued on page 252*

*Mom's Favorite White Cake*

*Mom's Favorite White Cake, continued*

Prepare Strawberry Frosting and Fruit Filling. Place one layer on cake plate; spread top with Fruit Filling. Place second layer over filling. Frost top and sides with Strawberry Frosting. Place strawberries on top of cake, if desired. Refrigerate; allow cake to stand at room temperature 15 minutes before serving.
*Makes 12 servings*

## STRAWBERRY FROSTING

2 envelopes (1.3 ounces each) whipped topping mix
⅔ cup milk
1 cup (6 ounces) white chocolate chips, melted
¼ cup strawberry jam

Beat whipped topping mix and milk in medium bowl with electric mixer on low speed until blended. Beat on high speed 4 minutes until topping thickens and forms peaks. With mixer at low speed, beat melted chocolate into topping. Add jam; beat until blended. Chill 15 minutes or until spreading consistency.

## FRUIT FILLING

1 cup Strawberry Frosting (recipe above)
1 can (8 ounces) crushed pineapple, drained
1 cup sliced strawberries

Combine Strawberry Frosting, pineapple and strawberries in medium bowl; mix well.

# HERSHEY'S RED VELVET CAKE

♥ ♥ ♥

½ cup (1 stick) butter or margarine, softened
1½ cups sugar
2 eggs
1 teaspoon vanilla extract
1 cup buttermilk or sour milk*
2 tablespoons (1-ounce bottle) red food color
2 cups all-purpose flour
⅓ cup HERSHEY'S Cocoa
1 teaspoon salt
1½ teaspoons baking soda
1 tablespoon white vinegar
1 can (16 ounces) ready-to-spread vanilla frosting
   HERSHEY'S MINI CHIPS® Semi-Sweet Chocolate or
   HERSHEY'S Milk Chocolate Chips (optional)

*To sour milk: Use 1 tablespoon white vinegar plus milk to equal 1 cup.

1. Heat oven to 350°F. Grease and flour 13×9×2-inch baking pan.

2. Beat butter and sugar in large bowl; add eggs and vanilla, beating well. Stir together buttermilk and food color. Stir together flour, cocoa and salt; add alternately to butter mixture with buttermilk mixture, mixing well. Stir in baking soda and vinegar. Pour into prepared pan.

3. Bake 30 to 35 minutes or until wooden pick inserted in center comes out clean. Cool completely in pan on wire rack. Frost; garnish with chocolate chips, if desired.

*Makes about 15 servings*

# PINEAPPLE-COCONUT UPSIDE-DOWN CAKE

♥ ♥ ♥

- 2 tablespoons light corn syrup
- 6 tablespoons butter, softened, divided
- ½ cup firmly packed light brown sugar
- 2 tablespoons flaked coconut
- 1 can (8 ounces) sliced pineapple in light syrup, drained
- 1⅓ cups all-purpose flour
- 2 teaspoons baking powder
- ¼ teaspoon salt
- ¾ cup granulated sugar
- 1 egg
- 1 teaspoon vanilla
- ⅔ cup skim milk
- 10 tablespoons light whipped topping
  Additional pineapple slices for garnish (optional)

1. Heat corn syrup and 1 tablespoon butter until melted in small skillet over medium heat. Stir in brown sugar; cook over medium heat until mixture is bubbly. Pour mixture into ungreased 9-inch round cake pan; sprinkle coconut evenly over top. Arrange whole pineapple slices on top of coconut.

*continued on page 256*

*Pineapple-Coconut Upside-Down Cake*

*Pineapple-Coconut Upside-Down Cake, continued*

2. Preheat oven to 350°F. Combine flour, baking powder and salt in medium bowl. Set aside. Beat remaining 5 tablespoons butter in large bowl until fluffy; beat in granulated sugar, egg and vanilla. Add flour mixture to butter mixture alternately with milk, beginning and ending with flour mixture. Pour batter into cake pan with prepared topping.

3. Bake about 40 minutes or until cake springs back when touched lightly. Cool in pan on wire rack 2 to 3 minutes; loosen side of cake with knife and invert onto serving plate. Cut cake into wedges. Serve warm or cool, topped with whipped topping. Garnish with pineapple slices, if desired.

*Makes 10 servings*

*Grandma's Secret: This cake would make an excellent ending to a summer barbecue or any time you are in a tropical mood. Ice cold Piña Colladas would complement this dessert nicely.*

# SPICE CAKE WITH RUM CARAMEL SAUCE

♥ ♥ ♥

1 package DUNCAN HINES® Moist Deluxe Spice Cake
  Mix
¾ cup prepared caramel topping
1 tablespoon rum or water
1 teaspoon ground cinnamon
½ cup milk chocolate English toffee chips
  Whipped cream for garnish

Preheat oven to 350°F. Grease and flour 13×9-inch pan.

Prepare and bake cake as directed on package. Cool cake 10 minutes.
Combine topping, rum and cinnamon in small bowl. Spread over warm cake.
Top with chips. Serve warm with whipped cream, if desired.

*Makes 12 to 16 servings*

*Grandma's Secret: The best method to determine that a cake is done is to insert a toothpick or cake tester into the center of the cake; the cake is done if the pick comes out clean and dry.*

# CHOCA-COLA CAKE

♥ ♥ ♥

## CAKE

| | |
|---|---|
| 1¾ | cups granulated sugar |
| ¾ | cup CRISCO® Stick or ¾ cup CRISCO® all-vegetable shortening |
| 2 | eggs |
| 2 | tablespoons cocoa |
| 1 | tablespoon pure vanilla extract |
| ¼ | teaspoon salt |
| ½ | cup buttermilk or sour milk* |
| 1 | teaspoon baking soda |
| 2½ | cups all-purpose flour |
| 1 | cup cola soft drink (not sugar-free) |

## FROSTING

| | |
|---|---|
| 1 | box (1 pound) confectioners' sugar (3½ to 4 cups) |
| 6 | tablespoons or more cola soft drink (not sugar-free) |
| ¼ | cup cocoa |
| ¼ | cup CRISCO® Stick or ¼ cup CRISCO® all-vegetable shortening |
| 1 | cup chopped pecans, divided |

*To sour milk: Combine 1½ teaspoons white vinegar plus enough milk to equal ½ cup. Stir. Wait 5 minutes before using.

*continued on page 260*

*Choca-Cola Cake*

*Choca-Cola Cake, continued*

1. Heat oven to 350°F. Line bottom of 13×9×2-inch baking pan with waxed paper.

2. **For cake,** combine granulated sugar and ¾ cup shortening in large bowl. Beat at medium speed of electric mixer 1 minute. Add eggs. Beat until blended. Add 2 tablespoons cocoa, vanilla and salt. Beat until blended.

3. Combine buttermilk and baking soda in small bowl. Add to creamed mixture. Beat until blended. Reduce speed to low. Add flour alternately with 1 cup cola, beginning and ending with flour, beating at low speed after each addition until well blended. Pour into pan.

4. Bake at 350°F for 30 to 35 minutes or until cake begins to pull away from sides of pan. *Do not overbake.* Cool 10 minutes before removing from pan. Invert cake on wire rack. Remove waxed paper. Cool completely. Place cake on serving tray.

5. **For frosting,** combine confectioners' sugar, 6 tablespoons cola, ¼ cup cocoa and ¼ cup shortening in medium bowl. Beat at low, then medium speed until blended, adding more cola, if necessary, until of desired spreading consistency. Stir in ½ cup nuts. Frost top and sides of cake. Sprinkle remaining nuts over top of cake. Let stand at least 1 hour before serving.          *Makes one 13×9×2-inch Cake (12 to 16 Servings)*

**Note:** Flavor of cake improves if made several hours or a day before serving.

# SOUR CREAM POUND CAKE

❤ ❤ ❤

  1  orange
  1  cup (2 sticks) butter, softened
2¾  cups sugar
  1  tablespoon vanilla
  6  eggs
  3  cups all-purpose flour
  ½  teaspoon salt
  ¼  teaspoon baking soda
  1  cup sour cream
     Citrus Topping (page 262)

Preheat oven to 325°F. Grease 10-inch tube pan. Finely grate colored peel, not white pith, from orange. Measure 2 teaspoons orange peel; set aside. Beat butter with electric mixer at medium speed in large bowl until creamy, scraping down side of bowl once. Gradually add sugar, beating until light and fluffy. Beat in vanilla and orange peel. Add eggs, one at a time, beating 1 minute after each addition. Combine flour, salt and baking soda in small bowl. Add to butter mixture alternately with sour cream, beginning and ending with flour mixture. Beat well after each addition. Pour into prepared pan. Bake 1 hour and 15 minutes or until cake tester or toothpick inserted in center comes out clean.

Meanwhile, prepare Citrus Topping. Spoon over hot cake; cool in pan 15 minutes. Remove from pan to wire rack; cool completely.

*Makes 10 to 12 servings*

*continued on page 262*

## CITRUS TOPPING

  2  **oranges**
  2  **teaspoons salt**
     **Water**
  ½  **cup sugar, divided**
  ⅓  **cup lemon juice**
  1  **teaspoon vanilla**

Finely grate colored peel, not white pith, from oranges. Measure ⅓ cup orange peel. Cut oranges in half. Squeeze juice from oranges into measuring cup or small bowl. Measure ⅓ cup orange juice. Combine orange peel and salt in medium saucepan. Add enough water to cover. Bring to a boil over high heat. Boil 2 minutes. Drain in fine-meshed sieve. Return orange peel to saucepan. Add orange juice and ¼ cup sugar to saucepan. Bring to a boil over high heat. Reduce heat; simmer 10 minutes. Remove from heat. Add remaining ¼ cup sugar, lemon juice and vanilla; stir until smooth.

*Sour Cream Pound Cake*

# CHOCOLATE CREAM-FILLED CAKE ROLL

♥ ♥ ♥

- ¾ cup sifted cake flour
- ¼ cup unsweetened cocoa
- ½ teaspoon baking powder
- ¼ teaspoon salt
- 4 eggs
- ¾ cup granulated sugar
- 1 tablespoon water
- 1 teaspoon vanilla extract
  Powdered sugar
  Cream Filling (page 266)
  Chocolate Stars (page 266)
  Sweetened whipped cream

Preheat oven to 375°F. Grease bottom of 15½×10½×1-inch jelly-roll pan. Line with waxed paper. Grease paper and sides of pan; dust with flour. Combine flour, cocoa, baking powder and salt in small bowl; set aside. Beat eggs in medium bowl at high speed about 5 minutes or until thick and lemon colored. Add granulated sugar, a little at a time, beating well at medium speed; beat until thick and fluffy. Stir in water and vanilla. Fold in flour mixture at low speed until smooth. Spread evenly in prepared pan.

Bake 12 to 15 minutes or until toothpick inserted in center comes out clean.

Meanwhile, sprinkle towel with powdered sugar. Loosen cake edges and turn out onto prepared towel.

*continued on page 266*

*Chocolate Cream-Filled Cake Roll*

*Chocolate Cream-Filled Cake Roll, continued*

Meanwhile, sprinkle towel with powdered sugar. Loosen cake edges and turn out onto prepared towel. Carefully peel off waxed paper. Roll up cake with towel inside, starting with narrow end. Cool, seam side down, 20 minutes on wire rack. Prepare Cream Filling and Chocolate Stars. Unroll cake and spread with Cream Filling. Roll up again, without towel. Cover and refrigerate at least 1 hour before serving. Dust with additional powdered sugar before serving. Place star tip in pastry bag; add sweetened whipped cream. Pipe rosettes on top of cake. Place points of Chocolate Stars in rosettes. Store tightly covered in refrigerator.          *Makes 8 to 10 servings*

## CREAM FILLING

> 1  **teaspoon unflavored gelatin**
> ¼  **cup cold water**
> 1  **cup whipping cream**
> 2  **tablespoons powdered sugar**
> 1  **tablespoon orange-flavored liqueur**

Sprinkle gelatin over cold water in small saucepan; let stand 1 minute to soften. Heat over low heat until dissolved, stirring constantly. Cool to room temperature. Beat cream, powdered sugar and liqueur in chilled bowl until stiff peaks form. Beat in gelatin mixture. Cover and refrigerate 5 to 10 minutes.

**Chocolate Stars:** Melt 2 squares (1 ounce each) semisweet chocolate in small saucepan over low heat, stirring frequently. Pour onto waxed-paper-lined cookie sheet. Spread to ⅛-inch thickness with metal spatula. Refrigerate about 15 minutes or until firm. Cut out stars with cookie cutter. Carefully lift stars from waxed paper using metal spatula or knife. Refrigerate until ready to use.

# CHOCOLATE CARAMEL PECAN BARS

### ♥ ♥ ♥

2 cups (4 sticks) butter, softened, divided
½ cup granulated sugar, divided
1 egg
2¾ cups all-purpose flour
⅔ cup packed light brown sugar
¼ cup light corn syrup
2½ cups coarsely chopped pecans
1 cup semisweet chocolate chips

1. Preheat oven to 375°F. Grease 15×10-inch jelly-roll pan; set aside.

2. Beat 1 cup butter and granulated sugar in large bowl with electric mixer at medium speed until light and fluffy. Beat in egg. Add flour. Beat at low speed until just blended. Spread dough into prepared pan. Bake 20 minutes or until light golden brown.

3. Meanwhile, prepare topping. Combine remaining 1 cup butter, brown sugar and corn syrup in medium, heavy saucepan. Bring to a boil over medium heat stirring frequently. Boil 2 minutes without stirring. Quickly stir in pecans; spread over base. Bake 20 minutes or until dark golden brown and bubbling.

4. Immediately sprinkle chocolate chips evenly over hot caramel. Gently press chips into caramel topping with spatula. Loosen caramel from edges of pan with spatula or knife. Remove pan to wire rack; cool completely. Cut into 3×1½-inch bars. Store tightly covered at room temperature or freeze up to 3 months.

*Makes 40 bars*

# OATMEAL SCOTCHIES™

♥ ♥ ♥

1¼ cups all-purpose flour
1 teaspoon baking soda
½ teaspoon salt
½ teaspoon ground cinnamon
1 cup (2 sticks) butter or margarine, softened
¾ cup granulated sugar
¾ cup packed brown sugar
2 eggs
1 teaspoon vanilla extract *or* grated peel of 1 orange
3 cups quick or old-fashioned oats
1⅔ cups (11-ounce package) NESTLÉ® TOLL HOUSE® Butterscotch Flavored Morsels

**COMBINE** flour, baking soda, salt and cinnamon in small bowl. Beat butter, granulated sugar, brown sugar, eggs and vanilla in large mixer bowl. Gradually beat in flour mixture. Stir in oats and morsels. Drop by rounded tablespoon onto ungreased baking sheets.

**BAKE** in preheated 375°F. oven for 7 to 8 minutes for chewy cookies; 9 to 10 minutes for crisp cookies. Cool on baking sheets for 2 minutes; remove to wire racks to cool completely. *Makes about 4 dozen cookies*

**Oatmeal Scotchie™ Pan Cookies:** SPREAD dough into greased 15½×10½-inch jelly-roll pan. Bake in preheated 375°F. oven for 18 to 22 minutes or until very lightly browned. Cool completely on wire rack. Makes 4 dozen bars.

*Oatmeal Scotchies™*

# FAVORITE MINI KISSES® COOKIES

♥ ♥ ♥

½ cup (1 stick) butter or margarine, softened
½ cup shortening
1 cup packed light brown sugar
½ cup granulated sugar
½ teaspoon baking soda
2 eggs
1 teaspoon vanilla extract
2½ cups all-purpose flour
1¾ cups (10-ounce package) HERSHEY'S MINI KISSES®
   Milk Chocolate Baking Pieces
1 cup chopped pecans or walnuts (optional)

1. Heat oven to 375°F. Beat butter and shortening in large bowl on medium speed of mixer just until blended.

2. Add brown sugar, granulated sugar and baking soda; beat until well blended. Add eggs and vanilla; beat well. Beat in flour (if dough becomes too stiff to beat in all with mixer, stir in remaining flour with spoon). Stir in Mini Kisses® and pecans, if desired. Using ¼ cup measure, drop dough about 4 inches apart onto ungreased cookie sheet.

3. Bake 10 to 12 minutes or until edges are lightly browned. Remove from cookie sheet to wire rack. Cool completely.          *Makes about 20 cookies*

# BAKER'S® ALMOND TOFFEE SQUARES

♥ ♥ ♥

- 1 cup (2 sticks) butter *or* margarine, softened
- 1 cup firmly packed brown sugar
- 1 egg
- 1 teaspoon vanilla
- 2 cups flour
- ¼ teaspoon salt
- 2 packages (4 ounces each) BAKER'S® GERMAN'S® Sweet Baking Chocolate, broken into squares
- ½ cup BAKER'S® ANGEL FLAKE® Coconut, lightly toasted
- ½ cup toasted slivered almonds

**HEAT** oven to 350°F.

**BEAT** butter, brown sugar, egg and vanilla. Stir in flour and salt. Press into greased foil lined 13×9-inch pan.

**BAKE** 30 minutes or until edges are golden brown. Remove from oven. Immediately place chocolate pieces on top. Cover with foil. Let stand 5 minutes or until chocolate is softened.

**SPREAD** chocolate evenly over entire surface. Sprinkle with coconut and almonds. Cut into squares while still warm; cool.          *Makes 32 squares*

**Prep Time:** 10 minutes
**Bake Time:** 30 minutes

# ALMOND BISCOTTI

❤ ❤ ❤

¼ **cup finely chopped slivered almonds**
½ **cup sugar**
2 **tablespoons butter**
4 **egg whites, lightly beaten**
2 **teaspoons almond extract**
2 **cups all-purpose flour**
2 **teaspoons baking powder**
¼ **teaspoon salt**

1. Preheat oven to 375°F. Place almonds in small baking pan. Bake 7 to 8 minutes or until golden brown. Set aside.

2. Beat sugar and butter in medium bowl with electric mixer until smooth. Add egg whites and almond extract; mix well. Combine flour, baking powder and salt in large bowl; mix well. Stir egg white mixture and almonds into flour mixture until well blended.

3. Spray two 9×5-inch loaf pans with nonstick cooking spray. Evenly divide dough between prepared pans; spread dough evenly onto bottoms of pans with wet fingertips. Bake 15 minutes or until knife inserted in centers comes out clean. Remove from oven; turn out onto cutting board.

4. As soon as loaves are cool enough to handle, cut each loaf into 16 (½-inch-thick) slices. Place slices on baking sheets sprayed with nonstick cooking spray. Bake 5 minutes; turn over. Bake 5 minutes more or until golden brown. Serve warm or cool completely. *Makes 32 biscotti*

*Almond Biscotti*

# CHOCOLATE MOUSSE SQUARES

❤ ❤ ❤

¾ cup plus 2 tablespoons all-purpose flour, divided
⅔ cup plus 3 tablespoons granulated sugar, divided
¼ cup (½ stick) cold margarine
¼ cup HERSHEY'S Cocoa
½ teaspoon powdered instant coffee
¼ teaspoon baking powder
½ cup liquid egg substitute
½ teaspoon vanilla extract
½ cup plain lowfat yogurt
½ teaspoon powdered sugar

1. Heat oven to 350°F. Stir together ¾ cup flour and 3 tablespoons granulated sugar in medium bowl. Cut in margarine, with pastry blender or 2 knives, until fine crumbs form. Press mixture onto bottom of ungreased 8-inch square baking pan.

2. Bake 15 minutes or until golden. *Reduce oven temperature to 300°F.*

3. Meanwhile, stir together remaining ⅔ cup granulated sugar, cocoa, remaining 2 tablespoons flour, instant coffee and baking powder in medium mixer bowl. Add egg substitute and vanilla; beat on medium speed of electric mixer until well blended. Add yogurt; beat just until blended. Pour over prepared crust.

4. Bake 30 minutes or until center is set. Cool completely in pan on wire rack. Cut into squares. If desired, place small paper cutouts over top. Sift powdered sugar over cutouts. Carefully remove cutouts. Store, covered, in refrigerator.

*Makes 16 squares*

# CHOCOLATE TASSIES

♥ ♥ ♥

**PASTRY**
- 2 cups all-purpose flour
- 2 packages (3 ounces each) cold cream cheese, cut into chunks
- 1 cup (2 sticks) cold butter, cut into chunks

**FILLING**
- 2 tablespoons butter
- 2 squares (1 ounce each) unsweetened chocolate
- 1½ cups packed brown sugar
- 2 eggs, beaten
- 2 teaspoons vanilla
- Dash salt
- 1½ cups chopped pecans

Place flour in large bowl. Cut in cream cheese and butter. Continue to mix until dough can be shaped into a ball. Wrap dough in plastic wrap; refrigerate 1 hour. Shape dough into 1-inch balls. Press each ball into ungreased miniature (1¾-inch) muffin pan cup, covering bottom and side of cup with dough.

Preheat oven to 350°F. Melt butter and chocolate in heavy medium saucepan over low heat. Remove from heat. Blend in brown sugar, eggs, vanilla and salt; beat until thick. Stir in pecans. Spoon about 1 teaspoon filling into each unbaked pastry shell. Bake 20 to 25 minutes or until pastry is lightly browned and filling is set. Cool in pans on wire racks. Remove from pans; store in airtight containers.

*Makes about 5 dozen cookies*

# CHOCOLATE X AND O COOKIES

♥ ♥ ♥

2/3 cup butter or margarine, softened
1 cup sugar
2 teaspoons vanilla extract
2 eggs
2 tablespoons light corn syrup
2½ cups all-purpose flour
½ cup HERSHEY'S Cocoa
½ teaspoon baking soda
¼ teaspoon salt
Decorating icing

1. Beat butter, sugar and vanilla in large bowl on medium speed of mixer until fluffy. Add eggs; beat well. Beat in corn syrup.

2. Combine flour, cocoa, baking soda and salt; gradually add to butter mixture, beating until well blended. Cover; refrigerate until dough is firm enough to handle.

3. Heat oven to 350°F. Shape dough into X and O shapes.* Place on ungreased cookie sheet.

4. Bake 5 minutes or until set. Remove from cookie sheet to wire rack. Cool completely. Decorate as desired with icing.     *Makes about 5 dozen cookies*

*To shape X's: Shape rounded teaspoons of dough into 3-inch logs. Place 1 log on cookie sheet; press lightly in center. Place another 3-inch log on top of first one, forming X shape. To shape O's: Shape rounded teaspoon dough into 5-inch logs. Connect ends, pressing lightly, forming O shape.

*Chocolate X and O Cookies*

# CHOCOLATE AND PEANUT BUTTER HEARTS

♥ ♥ ♥

1 recipe Chocolate Cookie Dough (page 280)
½ cup creamy peanut butter
½ cup shortening
1 cup sugar
1 egg
1 teaspoon vanilla
3 tablespoons milk
2 cups all-purpose flour
1 teaspoon baking powder
¼ teaspoon salt

1. Prepare Chocolate Cookie Dough. Divide dough in half; wrap in plastic wrap. Refrigerate about 2 hours or until firm.

2. Beat peanut butter, shortening and sugar at medium speed of electric mixer until fluffy. Add egg and vanilla; mix until well blended. Add milk; mix well.

3. Combine flour, baking powder and salt in medium bowl. Add flour mixture to peanut butter mixture; mix at low speed until well blended. Divide dough in half; wrap in plastic wrap. Refrigerate 1 to 2 hours or until firm.

4. Preheat oven to 350°F. Grease cookie sheets. Roll ½ of peanut butter dough on floured waxed paper to ⅛-inch thickness. Cut out cookies using 3-inch heart-shaped cookie cutter. Place on prepared cookie sheets.

*continued on page 280*

*Chocolate and Peanut Butter Hearts*

*Chocolate and Peanut Butter Hearts, continued*

5. Use smaller heart-shaped cookie cutter to remove small section from center of heart; set smaller cutouts aside.

6. Repeat with chocolate dough. Place small hearts into opposite dough according to photo; press lightly.

7. Bake 12 to 14 minutes or until edges are lightly browned. Remove to wire racks; cool completely.                      *Makes 4 dozen cookies*

## CHOCOLATE COOKIE DOUGH

    1  **cup (2 sticks) butter, softened**
    1  **cup sugar**
    1  **egg**
    1  **teaspoon vanilla**
    2  **ounces semisweet chocolate, melted**
 2¼  **cups all-purpose flour**
    1  **teaspoon baking powder**
  ¼  **teaspoon salt**

1. Beat butter and sugar in large bowl with electric mixer at high speed until fluffy. Beat in egg and vanilla. Add melted chocolate; mix well.

2. Add flour, baking powder and salt; mix well. Cover; refrigerate about 2 hours or until firm.

# MISSISSIPPI MUD BARS

♥ ♥ ♥

¾ cup packed brown sugar
½ cup (1 stick) butter, softened
1 egg
1 teaspoon vanilla
½ teaspoon baking soda
¼ teaspoon salt
1 cup plus 2 tablespoons all-purpose flour
1 cup (6 ounces) semisweet chocolate chips, divided
1 cup (6 ounces) white chocolate chips, divided
½ cup chopped walnuts or pecans

Preheat oven to 375°F. Line a 9-inch square pan with foil; grease foil. Beat sugar and butter in large bowl until blended and smooth. Beat in egg and vanilla until light. Blend in baking soda and salt. Add flour, mixing until well blended. Stir in ¾ cup each semisweet and white chocolate chips and nuts. Spread dough in prepared pan. Bake 23 to 25 minutes or until center feels firm. *Do not overbake.* Remove from oven; sprinkle remaining ¼ cup each semisweet and white chocolate chips over top. Let stand until chips melt; spread evenly over bars. Cool in pan on wire rack until chocolate is set. Cut into 2¼×1-inch bars.                    *Makes about 3 dozen bars*

# Pies & Tarts

## APPLE & CHERRY PIE

❤ ❤ ❤

- 2 cups all-purpose flour
- ½ cup plus 2 tablespoons sugar, divided
- ½ teaspoon salt
- 3 tablespoons *each* butter and vegetable shortening
- 1 tablespoon cider vinegar
- 5 to 6 tablespoons ice water
- ½ cup dried cherries
- ¼ cup apple juice
- 1 tablespoon cornstarch
- 2 teaspoons cinnamon
- 6 cups Jonagold or golden delicious apples, peeled and thinly sliced
- 1 teaspoon vanilla
  Glaze (optional)
- 1 egg white, well beaten
- 1 teaspoon sugar
- ¼ teaspoon cinnamon

*continued on page 284*

*Apple & Cherry Pie*

*Apple & Cherry Pie, continued*

1. Combine flour, 2 tablespoons sugar and salt in large bowl. Cut in butter and shortening with pastry blender or 2 knives until mixture resembles coarse crumbs. Add vinegar and 4 tablespoons water, stirring with a fork. Add additional ice water, 1 tablespoon at a time, until mixture forms a soft dough. Divide dough into thirds. Shape 1 piece into disk shape and wrap in plastic wrap. Combine remaining 2 pieces of dough forming larger disc shape; wrap in plastic wrap. Refrigerate 30 minutes.

2. Preheat oven to 375°F. In a small microwavable bowl, combine cherries and apple juice; microwave at HIGH 1½ minutes. Let stand 15 minutes to plump cherries. In a large bowl, combine remaining ½ cup sugar, cornstarch and cinnamon; mix well. Stir in apples, vanilla and cherries.

3. Coat 9-inch pie plate with nonstick cooking spray. Roll larger disc of dough to ⅛-inch thickness on a lightly floured surface. Cut into 12-inch circle. Transfer pastry to prepared pie plate. Spoon apple mixture into pastry. Roll smaller disc of dough to ⅛-inch thickness. Cut dough into ½-inch strips. Place strips over filling and weave into lattice design. Trim ends of lattice strips; fold edge of lower crust over ends of lattice strips. Seal and flute edge.

4. Brush pastry with egg white; sprinkle with combined sugar and cinnamon to glaze pie if desired. Bake 45 to 50 minutes or until apples are tender and crust is golden brown. Cool 30 minutes. Serve warm or at room temperature.

*Makes 8 servings*

# GINGER CREAM BANANA PIE

♥ ♥ ♥

1½ cups gingersnap cookie crumbs
¼ cup margarine, softened
2¼ cups milk
1 package (5.9 ounces) instant vanilla pudding
(6 servings)
1 tablespoon crystallized ginger
1 tablespoon grated orange peel
4 firm, medium DOLE® Bananas

• Combine gingersnap crumbs and margarine in bowl. Press on bottom and up side of 9-inch pie plate. Bake at 350°F 5 minutes. Cool.

• Combine milk, pudding, ginger and orange peel until well blended. Slice 2 bananas into bottom of pie shell. Cover with one-half filling. Slice remaining bananas over filling. Top with remaining filling. Press plastic wrap on surface. Refrigerate 3 hours. Garnish with additional banana slices, orange curls and edible flowers, if desired. *Makes 8 servings*

**Prep Time:** 25 minutes
**Chill Time:** 3 hours

# MOCHA ALMOND PIE

❤ ❤ ❤

1 KEEBLER® Ready Crust® Chocolate Pie Crust
1 (4-serving-size) package chocolate instant pudding and
    pie filling mix
1 tablespoon unsweetened cocoa powder
1 tablespoon instant coffee granules
1½ cups milk
2 cups whipped topping, thawed
½ cup toasted slivered almonds

In large bowl, combine pudding mix, cocoa and coffee granules.

Add milk; beat on low speed with electric mixer until thickened, about 2 minutes. Chill until set, about 5 minutes.

Fold whipped topping and almonds into pudding mixture, reserving 2 tablespoons mixture for garnish. Spread pudding mixture into crust. Freeze 1 to 2 hours.

Garnish with reserved almond mixture. *Makes 1 pie*

**Prep Time:** 15 minutes
**Chill Time:** 5 minutes
**Freeze Time:** 1 to 2 hours

*Mocha Almond Pie*

# PUMPKIN CHEESE-SWIRLED PIE

♥ ♥ ♥

1 package (3 ounces) cream cheese, softened
½ cup KARO® Light Corn Syrup, divided
½ teaspoon vanilla
1 cup canned solid pack pumpkin
2 eggs
½ cup evaporated milk
¼ cup sugar
2 teaspoons pumpkin pie spice
¼ teaspoon salt
   Easy-As-Pie Crust (page 290) or 1 (9-inch) frozen deep
   dish pie crust*

*To use prepared frozen pie crust: Use 9-inch deep-dish pie crust. Do not thaw. Preheat oven and a cookie sheet. Pour filling into frozen crust; bake on cookie sheet.

1. Preheat oven to 325°F.

2. In small bowl with mixer at medium speed, beat cream cheese until light and fluffy. Gradually beat in ¼ cup corn syrup and vanilla until smooth; set aside.

3. In medium bowl combine pumpkin, eggs, evaporated milk, remaining ¼ cup corn syrup, sugar, pumpkin pie spice and salt. Beat until smooth. Pour into pie crust.

*continued on page 290*

*Pumpkin Cheese-Swirled Pie*

*Pumpkin Cheese-Swirled Pie, continued*

4. Drop tablespoonfuls of cream cheese mixture onto pumpkin filling. With knife or small spatula, swirl mixture to give marbled effect.

5. Bake 50 to 60 minutes or until knife inserted halfway between edge and center comes out clean. Cool completely on wire rack.

*Makes 8 servings*

**Prep Time:** 20 minutes
**Bake Time:** 50 to 60 minutes, plus cooling

## EASY-AS-PIE CRUST

1¼ **cups unsifted flour**
⅛ **teaspoon salt**
½ **cup (1 stick) cold MAZOLA® Margarine**
2 **to 3 tablespoons cold water**

1. In medium bowl, combine flour and salt. With pastry blender or 2 knives, cut in margarine until mixture resembles fine crumbs.

2. Sprinkle water over mixture while tossing to blend well. Press dough firmly into ball.

3. On lightly floured surface, roll into 12-inch circle. Fit loosely into 9-inch pie plate. Trim and flute edge. Fill and bake according to recipe.

*Makes 1 (9-inch) crust*

**Baked Pie Shell:** Preheat oven to 450°F. Pierce pie crust thoroughly with fork. Bake 12 to 15 minutes or until light golden brown.

# BLUEBERRY CRUMBLE PIE

♥ ♥ ♥

1 KEEBLER® Ready Crust® Graham Cracker Pie Crust
1 egg yolk, beaten
1 (21-ounce) can blueberry pie filling
¼ cup sugar
⅓ cup all-purpose flour
⅓ cup quick-cooking oats
3 tablespoons margarine, melted

Preheat oven to 375°F. Brush bottom and sides of crust with egg yolk; bake on baking sheet until light brown, about 5 minutes.

Pour blueberry pie filling into crust. In small bowl, combine sugar, flour and oats; mix in melted margarine. Spoon over pie filling.

Bake on baking sheet about 35 minutes or until filling is bubbly and topping is browned. *Makes 1 pie*

**Prep Time:** 15 minutes
**Bake Time:** 40 minutes

# RASPBERRY CHOCOLATE MOUSSE PIE

♥ ♥ ♥

40 chocolate wafer cookies, finely crushed
½ cup butter, melted
½ cup water
7 tablespoons sugar
5 egg yolks
6 squares (1 ounce each) semisweet chocolate, melted
    and cooled slightly
3 tablespoons raspberry-flavored liqueur (optional)
3½ cups thawed nondairy whipped topping
    Sweetened whipped cream, raspberries and mint leaves

Combine cookie crumbs and butter in medium bowl; mix well. Press onto bottom and 1 inch up side of 9-inch springform pan.

Combine water and sugar in medium saucepan. Bring to a boil over medium-high heat. Boil 1 minute.

Place egg yolks in large bowl. Gradually whisk in hot sugar mixture. Return mixture to medium saucepan; whisk over low heat 1 to 2 minutes or until mixture is thick and creamy. Remove from heat; pour mixture back into large bowl.

Whisk in melted chocolate and liqueur, if desired. Beat mixture until cool. Fold in whipped topping. Pour mixture into prepared crust. Freeze until firm. Allow pie to stand at room temperature 20 minutes before serving. Remove side of pan. Garnish with sweetened whipped cream, fresh raspberries and mint leaves.                    *Makes 10 servings*

*Raspberry Chocolate Mousse Pie*

# FRENCH APPLE PIE

♥ ♥ ♥

**CRUST**
 1  9-inch Classic CRISCO® Double Crust (page 297)

**NUT FILLING**
 ¾  cup ground walnuts
 2  tablespoons packed brown sugar
 2  tablespoons beaten egg
 1  tablespoon milk
 1  tablespoon butter or margarine, softened
 ¼  teaspoon vanilla extract
 ¼  teaspoon lemon juice

**APPLE FILLING**
 5  cups sliced peeled Granny Smith apples
     (about 1¾ pounds or 5 medium)
 1  teaspoon lemon juice
 ¾  cup granulated sugar
 2  tablespoons all-purpose flour
 1  teaspoon ground cinnamon
 1  teaspoon ground nutmeg
 ¼  teaspoon salt
 2  tablespoons butter or margarine

*continued on page 296*

*French Apple Pie*

*French Apple Pie, continued*

1. **For Crust,** prepare 9-inch Classic Crisco® Double Crust. Press bottom crust into 9-inch pie plate. Do not bake. Heat oven to 425°F.

2. **For nut filling,** combine nuts, brown sugar, egg, milk, 1 tablespoon butter, vanilla and ¼ teaspoon lemon juice. Spread over bottom of unbaked pie crust.

3. **For apple filling,** place apples in large bowl. Sprinkle with 1 teaspoon lemon juice. Combine granulated sugar, flour, cinnamon, nutmeg and salt. Sprinkle over apples. Toss to mix. Spoon over nut filling. Dot with 2 tablespoons butter. Moisten pastry edge with water.

4. Cover pie with top crust. Trim to one-half inch beyond edge of pie plate. Fold top edge under bottom crust. Flute. Cut slits into top crust to allow steam to escape. Bake at 425°F for 50 minutes or until filling in center is bubbly and crust is golden brown. Cover crust edge with foil, if necessary, to prevent overbrowning. Cool until barely warm or at room temperature before serving.                            *Makes 1 (9-inch) pie*

# 9-INCH CLASSIC CRISCO® DOUBLE CRUST

### ♥ ♥ ♥

**2** cups all-purpose flour
**1** teaspoon salt
**¾** CRISCO® Stick or ¾ cup CRISCO® all-vegetable
    shortening
**5** tablespoons cold water

1. Spoon flour into measuring cup and level. Combine flour and salt in medium bowl.

2. Cut in shortening using pastry blender or 2 knives until flour is blended to form pea-size chunks.

3. Sprinkle with water, 1 tablespoon at a time. Toss lightly with fork until dough forms a ball.

4. Divide dough in half. Press half of dough between hands to form a 5- to 6-inch "pancake." Flour rolling surface and rolling pin lightly. Roll dough into circle. Trim circle 1 inch larger than upside-down pie plate. Carefully remove trimmed dough. Set aside to reroll and use for pastry cut out garnish, if desired. Repeat with remaining half of dough.

*Makes 2 (9-inch) crusts*

# COUNTRY PECAN PIE

♥ ♥ ♥

Pie pastry for single 9-inch pie crust
1¼ cups dark corn syrup
4 eggs
½ cup packed light brown sugar
¼ cup butter or margarine, melted
2 teaspoons all-purpose flour
1½ teaspoons vanilla extract
1½ cups pecan halves

Preheat oven to 350°F. Roll pastry on lightly floured surface to form 13-inch circle. Fit into 9-inch pie plate. Trim edges; flute. Set aside.

Combine corn syrup, eggs, brown sugar and melted butter in large bowl; beat with electric mixer on medium speed until well blended. Stir in flour and vanilla until blended. Pour into unbaked pie crust. Arrange pecans on top.

Bake 40 to 45 minutes until center of filling is puffed and golden brown. Cool completely on wire rack. Garnish as desired.      *Makes one 9-inch pie*

*Country Pecan Pie*

# DOUBLE LAYER PUMPKIN PIE

### ♥ ♥ ♥

½ package (4 ounces) PHILADELPHIA® Cream Cheese, cubed, softened
1 tablespoon half-and-half or milk
1 tablespoon sugar
1 tub (8 ounces) COOL WHIP® Whipped Topping, thawed
1 prepared graham cracker crumb crust (6 ounces)
1 cup cold half-and-half or milk
2 packages (4-serving size) JELL-O® Vanilla Flavor Instant Pudding & Pie Filling
1 can (16 ounces) pumpkin
1 teaspoon ground cinnamon
½ teaspoon ground ginger
¼ teaspoon ground cloves

**BEAT** cream cheese, 1 tablespoon half-and-half and sugar in large bowl with wire whisk until smooth. Gently stir in 1½ cups of the whipped topping. Spread onto bottom of crust.

**POUR** 1 cup half-and-half into bowl. Add pudding mixes. Beat with wire whisk 1 minute. (Mixture will be thick.) Stir in pumpkin and spices with wire whisk until well blended. Spread over cream cheese layer.

**REFRIGERATE** 4 hours or until set. Garnish with remaining whipped topping and sprinkle with additional cinnamon.           *Makes 8 servings*

*Double Layer Pumpkin Pie*

# APPLE ALMOND PIE

❤ ❤ ❤

¾ **cup sugar, divided**
¼ **cup ARGO® or KINGSFORD'S® Corn Starch**
3 **eggs**
½ **cup (1 stick) MAZOLA® Margarine, melted**
½ **cup KARO® Light or Dark Corn Syrup**
¼ **teaspoon almond extract**
2 **cups peeled, chopped apples (about 2 large)**
1 **cup sliced or slivered almonds, toasted**
 **Easy-As-Pie Crust (recipe follows), unbaked**
1 **apple, peeled and thinly sliced (optional)**
 **Sliced almonds, toasted (optional)**

1. Preheat oven to 375°F. Reserve 2 tablespoons sugar.

2. In medium bowl combine remaining sugar and corn starch. Beat in eggs until well blended. Stir in margarine, corn syrup and almond extract.

3. Mix in chopped apples and almonds. Pour into pie crust.

4. If desired, garnish with apple slices arranged in a circle around edge of pie; fill center with additional toasted almonds. Sprinkle reserved sugar over top.

5. Bake 50 minutes or until puffed and set. Cool on wire rack.

*Makes 8 servings*

**Note:** All-purpose apples such as Gravenstein, Jonathan, McIntosh or Winesap are ideal for this pie. If you prefer a cooking apple, try Northern Spy, Greening or Rome Beauty, but add a few minutes to the baking time.

**Prep Time:** 20 minutes
**Bake Time:** 50 minutes, plus cooling

## EASY-AS-PIE CRUST

1¼ **cups unsifted flour**
⅛ **teaspoon salt**
½ **cup (1 stick) cold MAZOLA® Margarine**
2 **to 3 tablespoons cold water**

1. In medium bowl, combine flour and salt. With pastry blender or 2 knives, cut in margarine until mixture resembles fine crumbs.

2. Sprinkle water over mixture while tossing to blend well. Press dough firmly into ball.

3. On lightly floured surface, roll into 12-inch circle. Fit loosely into 9-inch pie plate. Trim and flute edge. Fill and bake according to recipe.

*Makes 1 (9-inch) crust*

**Baked Pie Shell:** Preheat oven to 450°F. Pierce pie crust thoroughly with fork. Bake 12 to 15 minutes or until light golden brown.

# GEORGIA PEACH PIE

♥ ♥ ♥

**CRUST**

    1  **Unbaked 10-inch Classic CRISCO® Double Crust**
       **(page 307)**

**FILLING**

    1  **can (29 ounces) yellow cling peaches in heavy syrup**
    3  **tablespoons reserved peach syrup**
    3  **tablespoons cornstarch**
    1  **cup sugar, divided**
    3  **eggs**
   ⅓  **cup buttermilk**
   ½  **cup butter or margarine, melted**
    1  **teaspoon vanilla**

**GLAZE**

    2  **tablespoons butter or margarine, melted**
       **Additional sugar**

1. Heat oven to 400°F.

*continued on page 306*

*Georgia Peach Pie*

*Georgia Peach Pie, continued*

2. **For Filling,** drain peaches, reserving 3 tablespoons syrup; set aside. Cut peaches into small pieces; place in large bowl. Combine cornstarch and 3 tablespoons sugar in medium bowl. Add 3 tablespoons reserved peach syrup; mix well. Add remaining sugar, eggs and buttermilk; mix well. Stir in ½ cup melted butter and vanilla. Pour over peaches; stir until peaches are coated. Pour filling into unbaked pie crust. Moisten pastry edge with water.

3. Cover pie with top crust. Fold top edge under bottom crust; flute with fingers or fork. Cut slits or designs in top crust to allow steam to escape.

4. **For Glaze,** brush top crust with 2 tablespoons melted butter. Sprinkle with additional sugar.

5. Bake at 400°F for 45 minutes or until filling in center is bubbly and crust is golden brown. *Do not overbake.* Cool to room temperature before serving.

*Makes 1 (10-inch) pie*

*Grandma's Secret*: To quickly and easily peel peaches, mark an "X" on the bottom of the peach with a paring knife. Place peaches in boiling water for about 30 seconds. Carefully remove the peaches from the boiling water with a slotted spoon and place them in a large bowl of ice water. The skins will begin to peel away in a few seconds.

# 10-INCH CLASSIC CRISCO® DOUBLE CRUST

♥ ♥ ♥

2⅔ cups all-purpose flour
1 teaspoon salt
¾ CRISCO® Stick or ¾ cup CRISCO® all-vegetable
 shortening
7 to 8 tablespoons cold water

1. Spoon flour into measuring cup and level. Combine flour and salt in medium bowl.

2. Cut in shortening using pastry blender or 2 knives until all flour is blended to form pea-size chunks.

3. Sprinkle with water, 1 tablespoon at a time. Toss lightly with fork until dough forms a ball. Divide dough in half.

4. Press dough between hands to form 5- to 6-inch "pancake." Flour rolling surface and rolling pin lightly. Roll both halves of dough into circle. Trim one circle of dough 1 inch large than upside-down pie plate. Carefully remove trimmed dough. Set aside to reroll and use for pastry cutout garnish, if desired.

5. Fold dough into quarters. Unfold and press into pie plate. Trim edge even with plate. Add desired filling to unbaked crust. Moisten pastry edge with water. Lift top crust onto filled pie. Trim ½ inch beyond edge of pie plate. Fold top edge under bottom crust. Flute. Cut slits in top crust to allow steam to escape. Follow baking directions given for that recipe.

*Makes 1 double crust*

# LEMON COCONUT SOUR CREAM PIE

❤ ❤ ❤

- 1 can (about 16 ounces) lemon pie filling
- 1 package (4-serving size) instant coconut cream pudding mix
- 1 cup sour cream
- ¾ cup milk
- 1 (6-ounce) ready-to-use graham cracker crust
- ¼ cup flaked coconut
  Aerosol nondairy whipped topping

1. Preheat oven to 325°F. Place pie filling, pudding mix, sour cream and milk in large bowl. Beat with electric mixer at medium speed 3 to 4 minutes or until smooth. Pour into crust. Refrigerate 15 minutes.

2. While pie is chilling, spread coconut on baking sheet. Bake 8 to 10 minutes or until golden brown; cool.

3. Cover edge of pie with whipped topping. Sprinkle with coconut.

*Makes 8 servings*

**Prep and Cook Time:** 15 minutes

*Lemon Coconut Sour Cream Pie*

# MOCHA ICE CREAM PIE

♥ ♥ ♥

2 cups coffee or vanilla ice cream, softened
1 prepared (9-inch) chocolate crumb pie crust
1 jar (12 ounces) hot caramel ice cream topping, divided
2 cups chocolate ice cream, softened
2 cups thawed nondairy whipped topping
1 English toffee bar (1.4 ounces), chopped

Spread coffee ice cream in bottom of pie crust. Freeze 10 minutes or until semi-firm.

Spread half of caramel topping over coffee ice cream. Spread chocolate ice cream over caramel. Freeze 10 minutes or until semi-firm.

Spread remaining caramel topping over chocolate ice cream. Spoon whipped topping into pastry bag fitted with star decorating tip. Pipe rosettes on top of pie. Sprinkle toffee over topping.

Freeze pie until firm, 6 hours or overnight. Remove from freezer. Allow pie to stand at room temperature 15 minutes before serving.

*Makes 8 servings*

*Mocha Ice Cream Pie*

# RUSTIC APPLE CROUSTADE

♥ ♥ ♥

1⅓ cups all-purpose flour
¼ teaspoon salt
2 tablespoons butter or margarine
2 tablespoons vegetable shortening
4 to 5 tablespoons ice water
⅓ cup packed light brown sugar
1 tablespoon cornstarch
1 teaspoon cinnamon, divided
4 cups Jonathan or MacIntosh apples, peeled and sliced
1 egg white, beaten
1 tablespoon granulated sugar

1. Combine flour and salt in small bowl. Cut in butter and shortening with pastry blender or two knives until mixture resembles coarse crumbs. Mix in ice water, 1 tablespoon at a time, until mixture comes together and forms a soft dough. Wrap in plastic wrap; refrigerate 30 minutes.

2. Preheat oven to 375°F. Roll out pastry on floured surface to ⅛-inch thickness. Cut into 12-inch circle. Transfer pastry to nonstick jelly-roll pan.

3. Combine brown sugar, cornstarch and ¾ teaspoon cinnamon in medium bowl; mix well. Add apples; toss well. Spoon apple mixture in center of pastry leaving a 1½-inch border. Fold pastry over apples, folding edges in gently and pressing down lightly. Brush egg white over pastry. Sprinkle remaining ¼ teaspoon cinnamon and granulated sugar evenly over tart. Bake 35 to 40 minutes or until apples are tender and crust is golden brown. Let stand 20 minutes before serving. *Makes 8 servings*

*Rustic Apple Croustade*

# EASY FRUIT TARTS

♥ ♥ ♥

12   **wonton skins**
    **Vegetable cooking spray**
2   **tablespoons apple jelly or apricot fruit spread**
1½   **cups sliced or cut-up fruit such as DOLE® Bananas,
    Strawberries, Raspberries or Red or Green Seedless
    Grapes**
1   **cup nonfat or low fat yogurt, any flavor**

• Press wonton skins into 12 muffin cups sprayed with vegetable cooking spray, allowing corners to stand up over edges of muffin cups.

• Bake at 375°F 5 minutes or until lightly browned. Carefully remove wonton cups to wire rack; cool.

• Cook and stir jelly in small saucepan over low heat until jelly melts.

• Brush bottoms of cooled wonton cups with melted jelly. Place two fruit slices in each cup; spoon rounded tablespoon of yogurt on top of fruit. Garnish with fruit slice and mint leaves. Serve immediately.

*Makes 12 servings*

*Easy Fruit Tarts*

# WHITE CHOCOLATE CRANBERRY TART

♥ ♥ ♥

1   refrigerated pie crust (half of a 15-ounce package)
1   cup sugar
2   eggs
¼   cup butter or margarine, melted
2   teaspoons vanilla
½   cup all-purpose flour
1   package (6 ounces) white chocolate baking bar, chopped
½   cup chopped macadamia nuts, lightly toasted*
½   cup dried cranberries, coarsely chopped

*Toast chopped macadamia nuts in hot skillet about 3 minutes or until fragrant.

1. Preheat oven to 350°F. Line 9-inch tart pan with removable bottom or pie pan with pie crust (refrigerate or freeze other crust for another use).

2. Combine sugar, eggs, butter and vanilla in large bowl; mix well. Stir in flour until well blended. Add white chocolate, nuts and cranberries.

3. Pour filling into prepared pan. Bake 50 to 55 minutes or until top of tart is crusty and deep golden brown and knife inserted in center comes out clean.

4. Cool completely on wire rack. Cover and store at room temperature until serving time.

*Makes 8 servings*

*White Chocolate Cranberry Tart*

# TROPICAL FRUIT COCONUT TART

♥ ♥ ♥

1 cup cornflakes, crushed
1 can (3½ ounces) sweetened flaked coconut
2 egg whites
1 can (15¼ ounces) pineapple tidbits in juice
2 teaspoons cornstarch
4 teaspoons sugar
1 teaspoon coconut extract (optional)
1 mango, peeled and thinly sliced
1 banana, thinly sliced

1. Preheat oven to 425°F. Coat 9-inch springform pan with nonstick cooking spray; set aside.

2. Combine cereal, coconut and egg whites in medium bowl; toss gently to blend. Place coconut mixture in prepared pan; press firmly to coat bottom and ½ inch up side of pan.

3. Bake 8 minutes or until edge begins to brown. Cool completely on wire rack.

4. Drain pineapple, reserving pineapple juice. Combine pineapple juice and cornstarch in small saucepan; stir until cornstarch is dissolved. Bring to a boil over high heat. Continue boiling 1 minute, stirring constantly. Remove from heat; cool completely. Stir in sugar and coconut extract. Combine pineapple, mango slices and banana slices in medium bowl. Spoon into pan; drizzle with pineapple sauce. Cover with plastic wrap and refrigerate 2 hours.

*Makes 8 servings*

*Tropical Fruit Coconut Tart*

# PEPPERIDGE FARM® LEMON MERINGUE TARTS

♥ ♥ ♥

1 package (10 ounces) PEPPERIDGE FARM® Frozen Puff
   Pastry Shells
1 package (3 ounces) lemon pudding mix
1 teaspoon grated lemon peel
2 egg whites
¼ cup sugar

1. Bake and cool pastry shells according to package directions.

2. Prepare pudding mix according to package directions for pie filling. Stir in lemon peel and cool to room temperature.

3. Spoon about *⅓ cup* pudding into each pastry shell. Preheat oven to 325°F.

4. In medium bowl place egg whites. Beat with electric mixer at high speed until frothy. Gradually add sugar, beating until soft peaks form. Spoon over pudding sealing edges. Place on baking sheet. Bake 12 minutes or until lightly browned. Remove from baking sheet and cool on wire rack.

*Makes 6 servings*

**Variation:** Substitute sweetened whipped cream *or* whipped topping for egg whites and sugar. Top each filled pastry shell with whipped cream. Garnish with lemon slices if desired. Serve immediately or cover and refrigerate until serving time.

**Bake Time:** 30 minutes
**Prep Time:** 20 minutes
**Cook Time:** 15 minutes

# SPICED PEAR TART

♥ ♥ ♥

      30 gingersnap cookies
      ½ cup chopped pecans
      ⅓ cup butter, melted
      1 cup sour cream
      ¾ cup half-and-half
      1 package (4-serving size) vanilla instant pudding mix
      2 tablespoons apricot brandy
      1 (16-ounce) can pear halves, drained and thinly sliced
      ⅓ cup packed dark brown sugar
      ¼ teaspoon ground ginger
      ¼ teaspoon ground cinnamon
      ⅛ teaspoon ground cloves

Preheat oven to 350°F. Combine gingersnaps and pecans in food processor or blender; process until finely crushed. Combine crumb mixture and butter in medium bowl. Press firmly onto bottom and up side of 10-inch quiche dish or 9-inch pie plate. Bake 7 minutes; cool completely on wire rack.

Combine sour cream and half-and-half in large bowl; beat until smooth. Whisk in pudding mix. Add apricot brandy; beat until smooth. Pour into prepared pie crust. Cover; refrigerate several hours or overnight.

Just before serving, preheat broiler. Arrange pear halves in overlapping circles on top of pudding mixture. Combine brown sugar, ginger, cinnamon and cloves in small bowl. Sprinkle evenly over pears. Broil 4 to 6 minutes or until sugar is melted and bubbly. (Watch carefully so sugar does not burn.) Serve immediately.                                    *Makes 6 to 8 servings*

# WARM CHOCOLATE STRAWBERRY CAKE TARTS

### ♥ ♥ ♥

⅓ package (10¾ ounces) frozen pound cake, thawed
¼ cup plus 2 tablespoons prepared hot fudge sauce
2 tablespoons Amaretto or coffee liqueur (optional)
6 to 8 strawberries, sliced
3 tablespoons strawberry jam, melted
Additional prepared hot fudge sauce
Toasted slivered almonds
Vanilla ice cream

1. Cut cake into 4 equal slices. Place 2 slices together, long sides touching, on cutting board. Cut out circle from cake slices using 3-inch cutter. Repeat with remaining 2 slices to make 2 circles total.

2. Combine ¼ cup plus 2 tablespoons hot fudge sauce and liqueur, if desired, in glass measure.

3. Microwave at HIGH 30 seconds. Divide sauce evenly between 2 plates; tilt plates to swirl sauce to rim. Arrange cake circles over sauce. Arrange strawberries in ovelapping circles over cake. Brush strawberries with jam.

4. Microwave tarts, one at a time, at HIGH 30 seconds or until warm. Top with additional hot fudge sauce and slivered almonds. Serve with ice cream.

*Makes 2 servings*

**Prep and Cook Time:** 12 minutes

*Warm Chocolate Strawberry Cake Tart*

# FRESH FRUIT TART

♥ ♥ ♥

1⅔ cups all-purpose flour
⅓ cup sugar
¼ teaspoon salt
½ cup butter or margarine, softened and cut into pieces
1 egg yolk
2 to 3 tablespoons milk
1 package (8 ounces) regular or reduced-calorie cream cheese, softened
⅓ cup strawberry jam
2 to 3 cups mixed assorted fresh fruit, such as sliced bananas, sliced kiwi, blueberries, sliced peaches, sliced plums, raspberries and halved strawberries
¼ cup apple jelly, melted
¼ cup toasted sliced unblanched almonds (optional)

1. Combine flour, sugar and salt in food processor or blender; process until just combined. Add butter. Process using on/off pulsing action until mixture resembles coarse crumbs. Add egg yolk and 2 tablespoons milk; process until dough leaves side of bowl. Add additional milk by teaspoons, if necessary. Shape dough into a disc. Wrap in plastic wrap and refrigerate 30 minutes or until firm.

*continued on page 326*

*Fresh Fruit Tart*

*Fresh Fruit Tart, continued*

2. Preheat oven to 350°F. Roll dough out on lightly floured surface to ¼-inch thickness. Cut 12-inch circle; transfer to 10-inch tart pan with removable bottom. Press lightly onto bottom and up side of pan; trim edges even with edge of pan. Bake 16 to 18 minutes or until light golden brown. Transfer to wire rack; cool completely.

3. Combine cream cheese and jam in small bowl; mix well. Spread evenly over cooled crust. Arrange fruit decoratively over cream cheese layer. Brush fruit with apple jelly. Sprinkle with almonds, if desired. Serve immediately or refrigerate up to 2 hours before serving. *Makes 8 servings*

*Grandma's Secret: This scrumptious tart calls for a variety of fresh fruits. For maximum flavor, choose ripe fruits that are in season. They will add a natural sweetness to the tart that can't be beat. To avoid discoloration of ripe fresh fruit, prepare the fruit as it is called for in the recipe.*

# APPLE-CRANBERRY TART

♥ ♥ ♥

1⅓ cups all-purpose flour
¾ cup plus 1 tablespoon sugar, divided
¼ teaspoon salt
2 tablespoons vegetable shortening
2 tablespoons butter
4 to 5 tablespoons ice water
⅓ cup dried cranberries
½ cup boiling water
2 tablespoons cornstarch
1 teaspoon ground cinnamon
4 medium baking apples, peeled, cored and sliced
Vanilla frozen yogurt (optional)

1. Combine flour, 1 tablespoon sugar and salt in medium bowl. Cut in shortening and butter with pastry blender or two knives until mixture forms coarse crumbs. Mix in ice water, 1 tablespoon at a time, until mixture comes together and forms a soft dough. Wrap in plastic wrap. Refrigerate 30 minutes.

2. Combine cranberries and boiling water in small bowl. Let stand 20 minutes or until softened.

*continued on page 328*

3. Preheat oven to 425°F. Roll out dough on floured surface to ⅛-inch thickness. Cut into 11-inch circle. If leftover dough remains, use scraps for decorating top of tart. Ease dough into 10-inch tart pan with removable bottom leaving ¼-inch dough above rim of pan. Prick bottom and sides of dough with tines of fork; bake 12 minutes or until dough begins to brown. Cool on wire rack. Reduce oven temperature to 375°F.

4. Combine remaining ¾ cup sugar and cinnamon in large bowl; mix well. Reserve 1 teaspoon mixture for sprinkling over top of tart. Add cornstarch to bowl; mix well. Add apples; toss well. Drain cranberries; add to apple mixture; toss well.

5. Arrange apple mixture attractively over dough. Sprinkle reserved teaspoon sugar mixture evenly over top of tart. Place tart on baking sheet; bake 30 to 35 minutes or until apples are tender and crust is golden brown. Cool on wire rack. Remove side of pan; place tart on serving plate. Serve warm or at room temperature with frozen yogurt, if desired.

*Makes 8 servings*

*Grandma's Secret*: This tart makes a wonderful treat on a cool autumn night. After all, autumn is the time of year when baking apples such as Granny Smith, Jonathan, Jonagold or Rome Beauty are most abundant and at their peak flavor

*Apple-Cranberry Tart*

# AUTUMN PEAR TART

♥ ♥ ♥

    **Reduced-Fat Pastry (recipe follows)**
3  **to 4 tablespoons sugar**
2  **tablespoons cornstarch**
3  **to 4 large pears, cut into halves, cored, pared and**
     **sliced**
1  **tablespoon lemon juice**
    **Ground cinnamon (optional)**
    **Ground nutmeg (optional)**
¼  **cup apple jelly, apricot spreadable fruit or honey, warm**

1. Preheat oven to 425°F. Roll out pastry on floured surface to ⅛-inch thickness. Ease pastry into 9-inch tart pan with removable bottom; trim edge. Pierce bottom of pastry with tines of fork; bake 15 to 20 minutes or until pastry begins to brown. Cool on wire rack.

2. Combine sugar and cornstarch in small bowl; mix well. Sprinkle pears with lemon juice; toss with sugar mixture. Arrange sliced pears on pastry. Sprinkle lightly with cinnamon and nutmeg, if desired.

3. Bake 20 to 30 minutes or until pears are tender and crust is browned. Cool on wire rack. Brush pears with jelly. Remove side of pan; place tart on serving plate.

*Makes 8 servings*

# REDUCED-FAT PASTRY

   1⅓  **cups cake flour**
    2  **tablespoons sugar**
   ¼  **teaspoon salt**
   ¼  **cup vegetable shortening**
   4  **to 5 tablespoons ice water**

Combine flour, sugar and salt in small bowl. Cut in shortening with pastry blender or two knives until mixture forms coarse crumbs. Mix in ice water, 1 tablespoon at a time, until mixture comes together and forms a soft dough. Wrap in plastic wrap. Refrigerate 30 minutes before using.

*Makes pastry for one (9-inch) tart*

*Grandma's Secret: Pears are ripened off the tree for better flavor. You will seldom find ripe pears at the produce counter. To ripen fresh pears, place them in a paper bag in a cool place until they give to slight pressure.*

# Holiday Favorites

## ROASTED TURKEY BREAST WITH CHERRY & APPLE RICE STUFFING

♥ ♥ ♥

3¾  cups water
3  boxes UNCLE BEN'S® Butter & Herb Long Grain &
   Wild Rice
½  cup butter or margarine, divided
½  cup dried red tart cherries
1  large apple, peeled and chopped (about 1 cup)
½  cup sliced almonds, toasted*
1  bone-in turkey breast (5 to 6 pounds)

*To toast almonds, place them on a baking sheet. Bake 10 to 12 minutes in preheated 325°F oven or until golden brown, stirring occasionally.

*continued on page 334*

*Roasted Turkey Breast with Cherry
& Apple Rice Stuffing*

*Roasted Turkey Breast with Cherry & Apple Rice Stuffing, continued*

1. In large saucepan, combine water, rice, contents of seasoning packets, 3 tablespoons butter and cherries. Bring to a boil. Cover; reduce heat to low and simmer 25 minutes or until all water is absorbed. Stir in apple and almonds; set aside.

2. Preheat oven to 325°F. Place turkey breast, skin side down, on rack in roasting pan. Loosely fill breast cavity with rice stuffing. (Place any remaining stuffing in greased baking dish; cover and refrigerate. Bake alongside turkey for 35 to 40 minutes or until heated through.)

3. Place sheet of heavy-duty foil over stuffing, molding it slightly over sides of turkey. Carefully invert turkey, skin side up, on rack. Melt remaining 5 tablespoons butter; brush some of butter over surface of turkey.

4. Roast turkey, uncovered, 1 hour; baste with melted butter. Continue roasting 1¼ to 1¾ hours, basting occasionally with melted butter, until meat thermometer inserted into center of thickest part of turkey breast, not touching bone, registers 170°F. Let turkey stand, covered, 15 minutes before carving.

*Makes 6 to 8 servings*

*Grandma's Secret: Cherries add flavor to both sweet and savory dishes. They are high in vitamins and minerals while low in calories and sodium. Cherries are available fresh, frozen, dried, canned or bottled in juice.*

# SIDE BY SIDE SOUTHERN STUFFING AND TURKEY

♥ ♥ ♥

1 (3-pound) BUTTERBALL® Boneless Breast of Young
   Turkey with Gravy Packet, thawed
   Vegetable oil
1 can (14½ ounces) chicken broth
½ cup chopped onion
½ cup chopped celery
4 tablespoons butter or margarine
4 cups packaged cornbread stuffing
1 can (16 ounces) sliced peaches, drained and coarsely
   chopped
½ cup chopped pecans

Spray small roasting pan with nonstick cooking spray. Place boneless breast on one side of roasting pan. Brush with vegetable oil. Combine chicken broth, onion, celery and butter in large saucepan; simmer 5 minutes over low heat. Add stuffing, peaches and pecans; lightly toss mixture. Place stuffing alongside boneless breast. Cover stuffing with foil. Bake in preheated 325°F oven 1 hour and 45 minutes or until internal temperature reaches 170°F. Let boneless breast stand 10 minutes for easy carving. Prepare gravy according to package directions. Serve turkey with gravy and stuffing.                          *Makes 6 servings*

**Preparation Time:** 15 minutes plus roasting time

# HOPPIN' JOHN SUPPER

♥ ♥ ♥

1 cup converted white rice
1 can (14½ ounces) chicken broth
¼ cup water
1 package (16 ounces) frozen black-eyed peas, thawed
1 tablespoon vegetable oil
1 cup chopped onions
1 cup diced carrots
¾ cup thinly sliced celery with tops
3 cloves garlic, minced
12 ounces lean fully cooked ham, cut into chunks
¾ teaspoon hot pepper sauce
½ teaspoon salt

1. Combine rice, chicken broth and water in large saucepan; bring to a boil over high heat. Reduce heat; cover and simmer 10 minutes. Stir in black-eyed peas; cover and simmer 10 minutes or until rice and peas are tender and liquid is absorbed.

2. Meanwhile, heat oil in large skillet over medium heat. Add onion, carrots, celery and garlic; cook and stir 15 minutes or until vegetables are tender. Add ham; heat through. Add hot rice mixture, pepper sauce and salt; mix well. Cover; cook over low heat 10 minutes or until heated through.

*Makes 6 servings*

*Hoppin' John Supper*

# PEPPER STUFFED FLANK STEAK WITH CHEF'S SIGNATURE STEAK SAUCE

♥ ♥ ♥

1   flank steak (about 1½ pounds)
    Salt and ground black pepper
2   cups thinly sliced bell peppers (green, red and/or
        yellow)
1   small onion, thinly sliced
    Chef's Signature Steak Sauce (page 340)

Lay steak flat on baking sheet lined with plastic wrap. Cover and freeze about 2 hours or until nearly firm. Place steak on cutting board. Hold large sharp knife parallel to steak. Carefully cut steak in half lengthwise. Thaw in refrigerator until steak can be rolled up easily. Sprinkle inside of each piece of meat with salt and black pepper. Arrange bell peppers and onion on meat, leaving ½-inch edge around meat. Tightly roll up jelly-roll style; tie with kitchen string or secure with toothpicks.*

Prepare Chef's Signature Steak Sauce; set aside. Place steak on oiled grid. Grill over medium-hot coals 25 minutes for medium doneness, turning often. Baste with some of Chef's Signature Steak Sauce during last 10 minutes of cooking. Remove string or toothpicks. Let steak stand 5 minutes. Slice steak diagonally. Serve with remaining sauce.                    *Makes 6 servings*

*Soak toothpicks in water 20 minutes to prevent burning.

*continued on page 340*

*Pepper Stuffed Flank Steak with Chef's
Signature Steak Sauce*

*Pepper Stuffed Flank Steak with Chef's Signature Steak Sauce, continued*

## CHEF'S SIGNATURE STEAK SAUCE

- ½ cup ketchup
- ¼ cup FRENCH'S® Worcestershire Sauce
- 1 to 2 tablespoons FRANK'S® REDHOT® Hot Sauce or to taste
- 2 cloves garlic, minced

Combine ingredients in small bowl; stir until smooth.               *Makes ¾ cup*

# BAKED HAM WITH SWEET AND SPICY GLAZE

❤ ❤ ❤

- 1 (8-pound) bone-in smoked half ham
  Sweet and Spicy Glaze (recipe follows)

Preheat oven to 325°F. Place ham, fat side up, on rack in roasting pan. Insert meat thermometer into thickest part of ham away from fat or bone. Roast ham in oven about 3 hours.

Prepare Sweet and Spicy Glaze. Remove ham from oven. Generously brush half of glaze over ham; return to oven 30 minutes longer or until meat thermometer registers 160°F. Remove ham from oven and brush with remaining glaze. Let ham stand about 20 minutes before slicing.

*Makes 8 to 10 servings*

## SWEET AND SPICY GLAZE

¾ cup packed brown sugar
⅓ cup cider vinegar
¼ cup golden raisins
1 can (8¾ ounces) sliced peaches in heavy syrup,
    drained, chopped and syrup reserved
1 tablespoon cornstarch
¼ cup orange juice
1 can (8¼ ounces) crushed pineapple in syrup, undrained
1 tablespoon grated orange peel
1 clove garlic, minced
½ teaspoon red pepper flakes
½ teaspoon grated fresh ginger

Combine brown sugar, vinegar, raisins and peach syrup in medium saucepan. Bring to a boil over high heat; reduce to low and simmer 8 to 10 minutes. In small bowl, dissolve cornstarch in orange juice; add to brown sugar mixture. Add remaining ingredients; mix well. Cook over medium heat, stirring constantly, until mixture boils and thickens. Remove from heat.

*Makes about 2 cups*

# RACK OF LAMB WITH DIJON-MUSTARD SAUCE

❤ ❤ ❤

1   **rack of lamb (3 pounds), all visible fat removed**
1   **cup finely chopped fresh parsley**
½   **cup Dijon mustard**
½   **cup soft whole wheat bread crumbs**
1   **tablespoon chopped fresh rosemary *or* 2 teaspoons
    dried rosemary**
1   **teaspoon minced garlic**
   **Fresh rosemary, lemon slices and lemon peel strips
   (optional)**

Preheat oven to 500°F. Place lamb in large baking pan. Combine parsley, mustard, bread crumbs, rosemary and garlic in small bowl. Spread evenly over top of lamb. Place in center of oven; cook 7 minutes for medium-rare. Turn off oven but do not open door for at least 30 minutes. Serve 2 to 3 chops on each plate, depending on size and total number of chops. Garnish with additional fresh rosemary, lemon slices and lemon peel strips, if desired.

*Makes 6 servings*

*Rack of Lamb with Dijon-Mustard Sauce*

# ROAST TURKEY WITH FRESH HERB STUFFING

♥ ♥ ♥

4 cups cubed fresh herb- or garlic-flavored breadsticks
1 turkey (8 to 10 pounds)
1 tablespoon butter
1½ cups sliced mushrooms
1 cup chopped onion
⅔ cup chopped celery
¼ cup chopped fresh parsley
2 tablespoons chopped fresh tarragon
1 tablespoon chopped fresh thyme
¼ teaspoon ground black pepper
¼ cup reduced-sodium chicken broth

1. Preheat oven to 350°F. Place cubed breadsticks on nonstick baking sheet. Bake 20 minutes to dry. Melt butter in large skillet. Add mushrooms, onion and celery. Cook and stir 5 minutes or until onion is soft and golden; remove from heat. Add parsley, tarragon, thyme, pepper and bread cubes; stir until blended. Gently mix chicken broth into bread cube mixture. Fill turkey cavities with stuffing.

2. Spray roasting pan with nonstick cooking spray. Place turkey, breast side up, in roasting pan. Bake in 350°F oven 3 hours or until meat thermometer inserted in thigh registers, not touching any bone, 180°F and juices run clear.

3. Transfer turkey to serving platter. Cover loosely with foil; let stand 20 minutes. Remove and discard skin. Slice turkey and serve with herb stuffing.

*Makes 10 servings*

*Roast Turkey with Fresh Herb Stuffing*

# OLD-FASHIONED HERB STUFFING

♥ ♥ ♥

6  pieces (8 ounces) whole wheat, rye or white bread
    (or a combination of breads), cut into ½-inch pieces
1  tablespoon butter or margarine
1  cup chopped onion
½  cup thinly sliced celery
½  cup thinly sliced carrot
1  cup canned fat-free reduced-sodium chicken broth
1  tablespoon chopped fresh thyme *or* 1 teaspoon dried
1  tablespoon chopped fresh sage *or* 1 teaspoon dried
½  teaspoon paprika
¼  teaspoon ground black pepper

1. Preheat oven to 350°F. Place bread on a baking sheet; bake 10 minutes or until dry.

2. Melt butter in large saucepan over medium heat. Add onion, celery and carrot; cover and cook 10 minutes or until vegetables are tender. Add broth, thyme, sage, paprika and pepper; bring to a simmer. Stir in bread pieces; mix well. Remove pan from heat; set aside.

3. Coat a 1½ quart baking dish with nonstick cooking spray. Spoon stuffing into dish. Cover and bake 25 to 30 minutes or until heated through.

*Makes 4 servings*

*Old-Fashioned Herb Stuffing*

# SWEET POTATO PUFFS

♥ ♥ ♥

2 pounds sweet potatoes
⅓ cup orange juice
1 egg, beaten
1 tablespoon grated orange peel
½ teaspoon ground nutmeg
¼ cup chopped pecans

1. Peel and cut sweet potatoes into 1-inch pieces. Place potatoes in medium saucepan. Add enough water to cover; bring to a boil over medium-high heat. Cook 10 to 15 minutes or until tender. Drain potatoes and place in large bowl; mash until smooth. Add orange juice, egg, orange peel and nutmeg; mix well.

2. Preheat oven to 375°F. Spray baking sheet with nonstick cooking spray. Spoon potato mixture into 10 mounds on prepared baking sheet. Sprinkle pecans on tops of mounds.

3. Bake 30 minutes or until centers are hot. Garnish, if desired.

*Makes 10 servings*

# COCOA MARBLE GINGERBREAD

### ♥ ♥ ♥

½ cup shortening
1 cup sugar
1 cup light molasses
2 eggs
1 teaspoon baking soda
1 cup boiling water
2 cups all-purpose flour
1 teaspoon salt
¼ cup HERSHEY'S Cocoa
½ teaspoon ground cinnamon
½ teaspoon ground ginger
¼ teaspoon ground cloves
¼ teaspoon ground nutmeg
Sweetened whipped cream (optional)

1. Heat oven to 350°F. Grease and flour 13×9×2-inch baking pan.

2. Beat shortening, sugar and molasses in large bowl until blended. Add eggs; beat well. Stir baking soda into water to dissolve; add to shortening mixture alternately with combined flour and salt, beating well after each addition. Remove 2 cups batter to medium bowl. Add cocoa; blend well. Add spices to remaining batter in large bowl. Alternately spoon batters into prepared pan; gently swirl with knife for marbled effect.

3. Bake 40 to 45 minutes or until wooden pick inserted into center comes out clean. Serve warm or at room temperature with sweetened whipped cream, if desired.                    *Makes 10 to 12 servings*

# CRANBERRY PECAN WREATH

♥ ♥ ♥

3½ to 4 cups all-purpose flour
⅓ cup sugar
1 package FLEISCHMANN'S® RapidRise™ Yeast
¾ teaspoon salt
½ cup milk
¼ cup water
⅓ cup butter or margarine
2 large eggs
Cranberry-Pecan Filling (page 352)
Orange Glaze (page 352)

In large bowl, combine 1½ cups flour, sugar, undissolved yeast, and salt. Heat milk, water and butter until very warm (120° to 130°F); stir into dry ingredients. Stir in eggs and enough remaining flour to make soft dough. Knead on lightly floured surface until smooth and elastic, about 8 to 10 minutes. Cover; let rest 10 minutes.

Roll dough to 30×6-inch rectangle; spread Cranberry-Pecan Filling over dough to within ½ inch of edges. Beginning at long end, roll up tightly, pinching seam to seal. Form into ring; join ends, pinching to seal. Transfer to greased large baking sheet. Cover; let rise in warm, draft-free place until doubled in size, about 45 to 60 minutes.

*continued on page 352*

*Cranberry Pecan Wreath*

*Cranberry Pecan Wreath, continued*

Bake at 350°F for 40 to 45 minutes or until done. Remove from pan; cool on wire rack. Drizzle with Orange Glaze. Decorate with additional cranberries, orange slices and pecan halves, if desired.      *Makes 1 (10-inch) coffeecake*

**Cranberry-Pecan Filling:** In medium saucepan, combine 1½ cups fresh or frozen cranberries, finely chopped; 1 cup firmly packed brown sugar; and ⅓ cup butter or margarine. Bring to a boil over medium-high heat. Reduce heat; simmer 5 to 7 minutes or until very thick, stirring frequently. Remove mixture from heat; stir in ¾ cup chopped pecans, toasted.

**Orange Glaze:** In small bowl, combine 1¼ cups sifted powdered sugar; 2 tablespoons butter or margarine, softened; 1 to 2 tablespoons milk; and 2 teaspoons freshly grated orange peel. Stir until smooth.

*Grandma's Secret: This delicious and decorative coffeecake makes an excellent holiday treat. It can be served as part of a festive brunch or alone as a quick holiday morning snack. You can even leave Santa a piece instead of the traditional Christmas cookies.*

# HOLIDAY RYE BREAD

♥ ♥ ♥

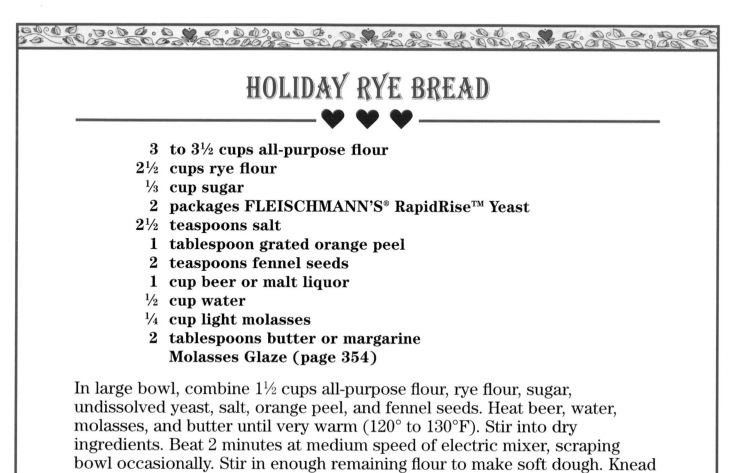

3 to 3½ cups all-purpose flour
2½ cups rye flour
⅓ cup sugar
2 packages FLEISCHMANN'S® RapidRise™ Yeast
2½ teaspoons salt
1 tablespoon grated orange peel
2 teaspoons fennel seeds
1 cup beer or malt liquor
½ cup water
¼ cup light molasses
2 tablespoons butter or margarine
  Molasses Glaze (page 354)

In large bowl, combine 1½ cups all-purpose flour, rye flour, sugar, undissolved yeast, salt, orange peel, and fennel seeds. Heat beer, water, molasses, and butter until very warm (120° to 130°F). Stir into dry ingredients. Beat 2 minutes at medium speed of electric mixer, scraping bowl occasionally. Stir in enough remaining flour to make soft dough. Knead on lightly floured surface until smooth and elastic, about 8 to 10 minutes. Cover; let rest 10 minutes.

*continued on page 354*

*Holiday Rye Bread, continued*

Divide dough into 4 equal pieces. Roll each to 10×6-inch oval. Roll each up tightly from long side, as for jelly roll, tapering ends. Pinch seams to seal. Place on greased baking sheets. Cover; let rise in warm, draft-free place until doubled in size, about 1½ hours.

With sharp knife, make 3 diagonals cuts on top of each loaf. Brush with Molasses Glaze. Bake at 375°F for 15 minutes; brush loaves with Glaze. Bake additional 10 minutes or until done. Remove loaves from oven and brush again with Glaze. Cool on wire racks.                    *Makes 4 small loaves*

**Molasses Glaze:** Combine 2 tablespoons molasses and 2 tablespoons water. Stir until well blended.

*Grandma's Secret: Rye flour is milled from rye grain and contains less gluten than wheat flour. It needs to be mixed with wheat flour, all-purpose or bread flour to produce a loaf that rises well and is not too dense. Rye flour is available in light, medium and dark varieties, with the medium variety being the most common.*

*Holiday Rye Bread*

# HOLIDAY CRANBERRY PUMPKIN BREAD

♥ ♥ ♥

**WESSON® No-Stick Cooking Spray**

## BREAD
- 2¼ cups sugar
- 1 cup canned or cooked fresh pumpkin
- ⅔ cup WESSON® Canola Oil
- 2 eggs, lightly beaten
- 1 tablespoon vanilla
- 2¼ cups all-purpose flour
- 1 cup chopped walnuts or hazelnuts (optional)
- 1 tablespoon pumpkin pie spice
- 1 teaspoon baking soda
- ½ teaspoon salt
- 2 cups coarsely chopped fresh cranberries

## GLAZE
- 1¼ cups powdered sugar
- 2 to 3 tablespoons warmed milk
- ⅔ cup coarsely chopped cranberries

Place rack in the middle of the oven. Preheat oven to 350°F. Spray two 8½×4½×2-inch loaf pans or one Bundt pan with Wesson® Cooking Spray.

*continued on page 358*

*Holiday Cranberry Pumpkin Bread*

**BREAD**

In medium bowl, combine sugar, pumpkin, Wesson® Oil, eggs and vanilla; mix well. In large mixing bowl, combine *remaining* bread ingredients *except* cranberries. Make a well in center of flour mixture; pour pumpkin mixture into center. Using wooden spoon, slowly blend flour mixture with pumpkin mixture. Mix until dry ingredients are moistened. Fold cranberries into batter; spoon into pans. Bake 1 hour or until wooden pick inserted into center comes out clean. Let bread cool 10 minutes on wire rack before removing from pan. Cool completely.

**GLAZE**

In small bowl, combine sugar and milk; mix until smooth. Fold ⅓ cup cranberries into glaze. Place bread on wire rack with wax paper under rack. Spoon glaze over bread to completely cover tops. Sprinkle *remaining* cranberries on top of glaze. Let glaze dry at least 20 minutes before serving.

*Makes 2 loaves or 1 Bundt bread*

*Grandma's Secret: Pumpkins are naturally good for you—high in fiber, Vitamin A and potassium. Fresh pumpkins are available from September through November. For baking purposes, choose smaller-sized pumpkins, known as cheese or sugar pumpkins. They have a sweet flesh that makes an excellent filling for pies and other baked goods.*

# CHOCOLATE SPRITZ

♥ ♥ ♥

  2  **squares (1 ounce each) unsweetened chocolate**
  1  **cup (2 sticks) butter, softened**
  ½  **cup granulated sugar**
  1  **egg**
  1  **teaspoon vanilla**
  ¼  **teaspoon salt**
  2¼  **cups all-purpose flour**
      **Powdered sugar**

Preheat oven to 400°F. Line cookie sheets with parchment paper or leave ungreased. Melt chocolate in top of double boiler over hot, not boiling, water. Remove from heat; cool. Beat butter, granulated sugar, egg, vanilla and salt in large bowl until light. Blend in melted chocolate and flour until stiff. Fit cookie press with your choice of plate. Load press with dough; press cookies out onto cookie sheets, spacing 2 inches apart.

Bake 5 to 7 minutes or just until very slightly browned around edges. Remove to wire racks to cool. Sprinkle with powdered sugar.

*Makes about 5 dozen cookies*

# HOLIDAY COOKIES ON A STICK

♥ ♥ ♥

1 cup (2 sticks) butter or margarine, softened
¾ cup granulated sugar
¾ cup packed light brown sugar
1 teaspoon vanilla extract
2 eggs
2⅓ cups all-purpose flour
½ cup HERSHEY'S Cocoa
1 teaspoon baking soda
½ teaspoon salt
  About 18 wooden ice cream sticks
1 tub (16 ounces) vanilla ready-to-spread frosting
  (optional)
  Decorating icing in tube, colored sugar, candy
  sprinkles, HERSHEY'S Holiday Candy Coated Bits,
  HERSHEY'S MINI KISSES® Semi-Sweet or Milk
  Chocolate Baking Pieces

1. Heat oven to 350°F.

2. Beat butter, granulated sugar, brown sugar and vanilla in large bowl on medium speed of mixer until creamy. Add eggs; beat well. Stir together flour, cocoa, baking soda and salt; gradually add to butter mixture, beating until well blended.

*continued on page 362*

*Holiday Cookies on a Stick*

*Holiday Cookies on a Stick, continued*

3. Drop dough by scant ¼ cupfuls onto ungreased cookie sheet, about 3 inches apart. Shape into balls. Insert wooden stick about three-fourths of the way into side of each ball. Flatten slightly.

4. Bake 8 to 10 minutes or until set. (Cookies will spread during baking.) Cool 3 minutes; using a wide spatula, carefully remove from cookie sheet to wire rack. Cool completely.

5. Spread with frosting, if desired. Decorate as desired with Christmas motifs, such as star, tree, candy cane, holly and Santa using decorating icing and garnishes.                              *Makes about 8 (3½-inch) cookies*

*Grandma's Secret: These festive cookies make great treats for a kids' Christmas party or make a fun family baking project. Make sure you have plenty of decorations on hand and let the creative juices flow.*

# FRIED NORWEGIAN COOKIES

♥ ♥ ♥

2 large eggs, at room temperature
3 tablespoons granulated sugar
¼ cup butter, melted
2 tablespoons milk
1 teaspoon vanilla
1¾ to 2 cups all-purpose flour
Vegetable oil
Powdered sugar

Beat eggs and sugar in large bowl with electric mixer at medium speed until thick and lemon colored. Beat in butter, milk and vanilla until well blended. Gradually add 1½ cups flour. Beat at low speed until well blended. Stir in enough remaining flour with spoon to form soft dough. Divided dough into 4 portions; cover and refrigerate until firm, at least 2 hours or overnight.

Working with floured hands, shape 1 portion dough at a time piece into 1-inch-thick square. Place dough on lightly floured surface. Roll out dough to 11-inch square. Cut dough into 1¼-inch strips; cut strips diagonally at 2-inch intervals. Cut a 1¼-inch slit vertically down center of each strip. Insert one end of strip through cut to form twist; repeat with each strip. Repeat with remaining dough.

Heat oil in large saucepan to 365°F. Place 12 cookies at a time in hot oil. Fry about 1½ minutes or until golden brown, turning cookies once with slotted spoon. Drain on paper towels. Dust cookies with powdered sugar. Cookies are best if served immediately, but can be stored in airtight container 1 day.

*Makes about 11 dozen cookies*

# WELSH TEA CAKES

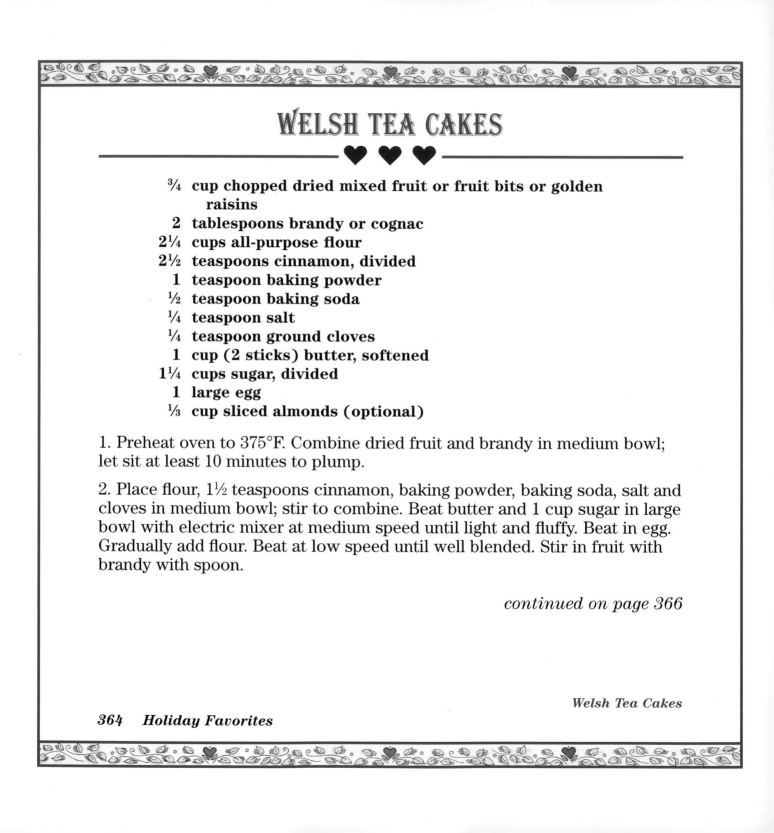

¾ cup chopped dried mixed fruit or fruit bits or golden
    raisins
2 tablespoons brandy or cognac
2¼ cups all-purpose flour
2½ teaspoons cinnamon, divided
1 teaspoon baking powder
½ teaspoon baking soda
¼ teaspoon salt
¼ teaspoon ground cloves
1 cup (2 sticks) butter, softened
1¼ cups sugar, divided
1 large egg
⅓ cup sliced almonds (optional)

1. Preheat oven to 375°F. Combine dried fruit and brandy in medium bowl; let sit at least 10 minutes to plump.

2. Place flour, 1½ teaspoons cinnamon, baking powder, baking soda, salt and cloves in medium bowl; stir to combine. Beat butter and 1 cup sugar in large bowl with electric mixer at medium speed until light and fluffy. Beat in egg. Gradually add flour. Beat at low speed until well blended. Stir in fruit with brandy with spoon.

*continued on page 366*

*Welsh Tea Cakes*

*Welsh Tea Cakes, continued*

3. Combine remaining ¼ cup sugar and 1 teaspoon cinnamon in small bowl. Roll heaping teaspoonfuls of dough into 1-inch balls; roll balls in cinnamon sugar to coat. Place balls 2 inches apart on ungreased cookie sheets.

4. Press balls to ¼-inch thickness using bottom of glass dipped in granulated sugar. Press 3 almond slices horizontally into center of each cookie. (Almonds will spread evenly and flatten upon baking.)

5. Bake 10 to 12 minutes or until lightly browned. Remove tea cakes with spatula to wire racks; cool completely.

6. Store tightly covered at room temperature or freeze up to 3 months.

*Makes about 3½ dozen cookies*

*Grandma's Secret: The traditional Welsh method for cooking these cakes is on a pan or griddle. In this version of the classic recipe, they are baked. Take a hint from the Welsh and take a few minutes out of your busy day to enjoy a hot cup of tea and a few of these deliciously sweet and spicy cakes.*

# AUTUMN GOLD PUMPKIN CAKE

❤ ❤ ❤

1 package DUNCAN HINES® Moist Deluxe Butter Recipe
    Golden Cake Mix
3 eggs
1 cup water
1 cup solid pack pumpkin
1½ teaspoons ground cinnamon, divided
¼ teaspoon ground ginger
¼ teaspoon ground nutmeg
1 cup chopped walnuts
1 container DUNCAN HINES® Vanilla Frosting
¼ cup coarsely chopped walnuts for garnish

Preheat oven to 375°F. Grease and flour two 8-inch round cake pans. Combine cake mix, eggs, water, pumpkin, 1 teaspoon cinnamon, ginger and nutmeg in large mixing bowl. Beat at medium speed with electric mixer for 4 minutes. Stir in 1 cup walnuts. Pour into prepared pans. Bake 30 to 35 minutes or until toothpick inserted in center comes out clean. Cool in pans 15 minutes. Remove from pans. Cool completely. Combine frosting and remaining ½ teaspoon cinnamon. Stir until blended. Fill and frost cake. Garnish with ¼ cup walnuts.                    *Makes 12 to 16 servings*

# MERRY CHERRY HOLIDAY DESSERT

❤ ❤ ❤

1½ cups boiling water
1 package (8-serving size) or 2 packages (4-serving size)
    JELL-O® Brand Cherry Flavor Gelatin Dessert, or any
    red flavor
1½ cups cold water
1 can (21 ounces) cherry pie filling
4 cups angel food cake cubes
3 cups cold milk
2 packages (4-serving size) JELL-O® Vanilla Flavor
    Instant Pudding & Pie Filling
1 tub (8 ounces) COOL WHIP® Whipped Topping, thawed

**STIR** boiling water into gelatin in large bowl at least 2 minutes until completely dissolved. Stir in cold water and cherry pie filling. Refrigerate about 1 hour or until slightly thickened (consistency of unbeaten egg whites). Place cake cubes in 3-quart serving bowl. Spoon gelatin mixture over cake. Refrigerate about 45 minutes or until set but not firm (gelatin should stick to finger when touched and should mound).

**POUR** milk into large bowl. Add pudding mixes. Beat with wire whisk 1 minute. Gently stir in 2 cups of the whipped topping. Spoon over gelatin mixture in bowl.

**REFRIGERATE** 2 hours or until set. Top with remaining whipped topping and garnish as desired. *Makes 16 servings*

**Preparation Time:** 20 minutes

*Merry Cherry Holiday Dessert*

# MINI KISSES® PUMPKIN MOUSSE CUPS

### ♥ ♥ ♥

1¾ cups (10-ounce package) HERSHEY'S MINI KISSES®
      Semi-Sweet Baking Pieces, divided
24 marshmallows
½ cup milk
½ cup canned pumpkin
1 teaspoon vanilla extract
1 teaspoon pumpkin pie spice
⅓ cup powdered sugar
1 cup (½ pint) cold whipping cream

1. Line 10 muffin cups (2½ inches in diameter) with paper bake cups. Reserve ½ cup Mini Kisses®. Place remaining 1¼ cups Mini Kisses® in small microwave-safe bowl; microwave at HIGH (100%) 1 minute or until melted when stirred. Mixture should be thick. Very thickly coat inside pleated surfaces and bottoms of bake cups with melted chocolate using soft pastry brush. Refrigerate 10 minutes; recoat any thin spots with melted chocolate. Refrigerate until firm, about 2 hours. Gently peel off paper; refrigerate until ready to fill.

2. Place marshmallows, milk, and pumpkin in medium microwave-safe bowl. Microwave at HIGH 1 minute; stir. Microwave additional 30 seconds at a time, stirring after each heating, until mixture is melted and smooth. Stir in vanilla and pumpkin pie spice. Cool completely. Beat powdered sugar and whipping cream until stiff; fold into pumpkin mixture. Fill cups with pumpkin mousse; garnish with reserved Mini Kisses®. Cover; refrigerate 2 hours or until firm. *Makes 10 servings*

*Mini Kisses® Pumpkin Mousse Cups*

# CRAN-RASPBERRY HAZELNUT TRIFLE

♥ ♥ ♥

2 cups hazelnut-flavored dairy creamer
1 package (4-serving size) instant vanilla pudding and
    pie filling mix
1 package (10¾ ounces) frozen pound cake, thawed
1 can (21 ounces) raspberry pie filling
1 can (16 ounces) whole berry cranberry sauce

1. Combine dairy creamer and pudding in medium bowl; beat with wire whisk 1 to 2 minutes or until thickened.

2. Cut pound cake into ¾-inch cubes. Combine pie filling and cranberry sauce in medium bowl; blend well.

3. Layer ⅓ of cake cubes, ¼ of fruit sauce and ⅓ of pudding mixture in 1½- to 2-quart straight-sided glass serving bowl. Repeat layers twice; top with remaining fruit sauce. Cover; refrigerate until serving time.

*Makes 8 servings*

**Prep Time:** 20 minutes

*Cran-Raspberry Hazelnut Trifle*

# Acknowledgments

*The publishers would like to thank the companies and organizations listed below for the use of their recipes and photographs in this publication.*

American Lamb Council

Bestfoods

Butterball® Turkey Company

California Table Grape Commission

Campbell Soup Company

Colorado Potato Administrative Committee

ConAgra Grocery Products Company

Del Monte Corporation

Dole Food Company, Inc.

Duncan Hines® and Moist Deluxe® are registered trademarks of Aurora Foods Inc.

Fleischmann's® Yeast

Grey Poupon® Mustard

Hebrew National®

Hershey Foods Corporation

Keebler Company

Kraft Foods, Inc.

Land O' Lakes, Inc.

Lawry's® Foods, Inc.

Lipton®

National Cattlemen's Beef Association

National Honey Board

National Turkey Federation

Nestlé USA, Inc.

North Dakota Beef Commission

Reckitt & Colman Inc.

Sargento® Foods Inc.

The Golden Grain Company®

The HV Company

The Kingsford Products Company

The Procter & Gamble Company

The Sugar Association, Inc.

Uncle Ben's Inc.

USA Rice Federation

# Index

# METRIC CONVERSION CHART

### VOLUME MEASUREMENTS (dry)

$1/8$ teaspoon = 0.5 mL
$1/4$ teaspoon = 1 mL
$1/2$ teaspoon = 2 mL
$3/4$ teaspoon = 4 mL
1 teaspoon = 5 mL
1 tablespoon = 15 mL
2 tablespoons = 30 mL
$1/4$ cup = 60 mL
$1/3$ cup = 75 mL
$1/2$ cup = 125 mL
$2/3$ cup = 150 mL
$3/4$ cup = 175 mL
1 cup = 250 mL
2 cups = 1 pint = 500 mL
3 cups = 750 mL
4 cups = 1 quart = 1 L

### VOLUME MEASUREMENTS (fluid)

1 fluid ounce (2 tablespoons) = 30 mL
4 fluid ounces ($1/2$ cup) = 125 mL
8 fluid ounces (1 cup) = 250 mL
12 fluid ounces ($1\frac{1}{2}$ cups) = 375 mL
16 fluid ounces (2 cups) = 500 mL

### WEIGHTS (mass)

$1/2$ ounce = 15 g
1 ounce = 30 g
3 ounces = 90 g
4 ounces = 120 g
8 ounces = 225 g
10 ounces = 285 g
12 ounces = 360 g
16 ounces = 1 pound = 450 g

### DIMENSIONS

$1/16$ inch = 2 mm
$1/8$ inch = 3 mm
$1/4$ inch = 6 mm
$1/2$ inch = 1.5 cm
$3/4$ inch = 2 cm
1 inch = 2.5 cm

### OVEN TEMPERATURES

250°F = 120°C
275°F = 140°C
300°F = 150°C
325°F = 160°C
350°F = 180°C
375°F = 190°C
400°F = 200°C
425°F = 220°C
450°F = 230°C

### BAKING PAN SIZES

| Utensil | Size in Inches/Quarts | Metric Volume | Size in Centimeters |
|---|---|---|---|
| Baking or Cake Pan (square or rectangular) | 8×8×2 | 2 L | 20×20×5 |
| | 9×9×2 | 2.5 L | 23×23×5 |
| | 12×8×2 | 3 L | 30×20×5 |
| | 13×9×2 | 3.5 L | 33×23×5 |
| Loaf Pan | 8×4×3 | 1.5 L | 20×10×7 |
| | 9×5×3 | 2 L | 23×13×7 |
| Round Layer Cake Pan | 8×1½ | 1.2 L | 20×4 |
| | 9×1½ | 1.5 L | 23×4 |
| Pie Plate | 8×1¼ | 750 mL | 20×3 |
| | 9×1¼ | 1 L | 23×3 |
| Baking Dish or Casserole | 1 quart | 1 L | — |
| | 1½ quart | 1.5 L | — |
| | 2 quart | 2 L | — |